MESOPOTAMIAN GODS & GODDESSES

GODS AND GODDESSES OF MYTHOLOGY

MESOPOTAMIAN GODS & GODDESSES

EDITED BY VINCENT HALE

IN ASSOCIATION WITH

EDUCATIONAL SERVICES

Published in 2014 by Britannica Educational Publishing (a trademark of Encyclopædia Britannica, Inc.) in association with The Rosen Publishing Group, Inc.
29 East 21st Street, New York, NY 10010

To see additional Britannica Educational Publishing titles, go to http://www.rosenpublishing.com

First Edition

Britannica Educational Publishing
J. E. Luebering: Director, Core Reference Group
Anthony L. Green: Editor, Compton's by Britannica

Rosen Publishing
Hope Lourie Killcoyne: Executive Editor
Vincent Hale: Editor
Nelson Sá: Art Director
Brian Garvey: Designer
Cindy Reiman: Photography Manager

Cataloging-in-Publication Data

Hale, Vincent.
Mesopotamian gods & goddesses/edited by Vincent Hale — 1st ed.
    p. cm.—(Gods & goddesses of mythology)
Includes index and bibliography.
ISBN 978-1-62275-161-7 (library binding)
1. Mythology, Assyro-Babylonian—Juvenile literature. 2. Civilization, Assyro-Babylonian—Juvenile literature. I. Title.
BL1620.H35 2014
299—d23

Manufactured in the United States of America

On the cover: *An ancient Mesopotamian relief.* jsp/Shutterstock.com

Interior pages (cuneiform) khd/Shutterstock.com

CONTENTS

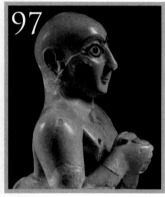

Assyrian wall illustration bearing cuneiform script. khd/Shutterstock.com

INTRODUCTION

M esopotamian religion and mythology were the beliefs and practices of the Sumerians and Akkadians, and their successors, the Babylonians and Assyrians, who inhabited ancient Mesopotamia (now in Iraq) in the millennia before the Christian era. These religious beliefs and practices form a single stream of tradition. Sumerian in origin, Mesopotamian religion was added to and subtly modified by the Akkadians (Semites who emigrated into Mesopotamia from the west at the end of the 4th millennium BCE), whose own beliefs were in large measure assimilated to, and integrated with, those of their new environment.

As the only available intellectual framework that could provide a comprehensive understanding of the forces governing existence and also guidance for right conduct in life, religion ineluctably conditioned all aspects of ancient Mesopotamian civilization. It yielded the forms in which that civilization's social, economic, legal, political, and military institutions were, and are, to be understood, and it provided the significant symbols for poetry and art. In many ways it even influenced peoples and cultures outside Mesopotamia, such as the Elamites to the east, the Hurrians and Hittites to the north, and the Aramaeans and Israelites to the west.

The genre of myths in ancient Mesopotamian literature centres on praises that recount and celebrate great deeds. The doers of the deeds (creative or otherwise decisive acts), and thus the subjects of the praises, are the gods. In the oldest myths, the Sumerian, these acts tend to have particular rather than universal relevance, which is understandable since they deal with the power and acts of a particular god with a particular sphere of influence in the cosmos. An example of such myths is the myth of "Dumuzi's Death," which relates how Dumuzi (Producer of Sound Offspring; Akkadian: Tammuz), the power in

A carved stone vessel known as the Uruk Vase, illustrating the Sumerian goddess Inanna, located in the city of Uruk in modern-day Iraq. Marc Deville/Gamma-Rapho/Getty Images

the fertility of spring, dreamed of his own death at the hands of a group of deputies from the netherworld and how he tried to hide himself but was betrayed by his friend after his sister had resisted all attempts to make her reveal where he was.

A similar, very complex myth, "Inanna's Descent," relates how the goddess Inanna (Lady of the Date Clusters) set her heart on ruling the netherworld and tried to depose her older sister, the queen of the netherworld, Ereshkigal (Lady of the Great Place). Her attempt failed, and she was killed and changed into a piece of rotting meat in the netherworld. It took all the ingenuity of Enki (Lord of Sweet Waters in the Earth) to bring Inanna back to life, and even then she was released only on condition that she furnish a substitute to take her place. On her return, finding her young husband Dumuzi feasting instead of mourning for her, Inanna was seized with jealousy and designated him that substitute. Dumuzi tried to flee the posse of deputies who had accompanied Inanna, and with the help of the sun god Utu (Sun), who changed Dumuzi's shape, he managed to escape, was recaptured, escaped again, and so on, until he was finally taken to the netherworld. The fly told his little sister Geshtinanna where he was, and she went in search of him. The myth ends with Inanna rewarding the fly and decreeing that Dumuzi and his little sister could alternate as her substitute, each of them spending half a year in the netherworld, the other half above with the living.

A third myth built over the motif of journeying to the netherworld is the myth of "The Engendering of the Moongod and his Brothers," which tells how Enlil (Lord of the Air), when still a youngster, came upon young Ninlil (goddess of grain) as she—eager to be with child and disobeying her mother—was bathing in a canal where he would see her. He lay with her in spite of her pretending to protest and thus engendered the moon god Su-en (Sin). For this offense Enlil was banished from Nippur and took the road to the netherworld. Ninlil, carrying his child, followed him. On the way Enlil took the shape first of the Nippur gatekeeper, then of the man of the river of the netherworld, and lastly of the ferryman of the river of the netherworld. In each such disguise Enlil persuaded Ninlil to let him lie with her to engender a son who might take Su-en's place in the netherworld and leave him free for the world above. Thus three additional deities, all underworld figures, were engendered: Meslamtaea (He Who Issues from Meslam), Ninazu (Water Knower), and Ennugi (the Lord Who Returns Not). The myth ends with a paean to Enlil as a source of abundance and to his divine word, which always comes true.

Most likely all of these myths have backgrounds in fertility cults and concern either the disappearance of nature's fertility with the onset of the dry season or the underground storage of food.

As Enlil is celebrated for engendering other gods that embody other powers in nature, so also was Enki in the myth of "Enki and Ninhursag," in which myth Enki lay with Ninhursag (Lady of the Stony Ground) on the island of Dilmun (modern Bahrain), which had been allotted to them. At that time all was new and fresh, inchoate, not yet set in its present mold. There Enki provided water for the future city of Dilmun, lay with Ninhursag, and left her. She gave birth to a daughter, Ninshar (Lady Herb), on whom Enki in turn engendered the spider Uttu, goddess of spinning and weaving. Ninhursag warned Uttu against Enki, but he, proffering marriage gifts, persuaded her to open the door to him. After Enki had abandoned Uttu, Ninhursag found her and removed Enki's semen from her body. From the semen seven plants sprouted forth. These plants Enki later saw and ate and so became impregnated himself. Unable as a male to give birth, he fell fatally ill, until Ninhursag relented and—as birth goddess—placed him in her and helped him to give birth to seven daughters, whom Enki then happily married off to various gods. The story is probably to be seen as a bit of broad humour.

Not only the birth of gods but also the birth, or creation, of the human race is treated in the myths. The myth of "Enki and Ninmah" relates how the gods originally had to toil for their food, dig irrigation canals, and perform other menial tasks until, in their distress, they complained to Enki's mother, Nammu, who took the complaints to Enki. Enki remembered the engendering clay of the Apsu (i.e., the fresh underground waters that fathered him), and from this clay, with the help of the womb goddesses and eight midwife goddesses led by Ninmah (another name for Ninhursag), he had his mother become pregnant with and give birth to humanity so that he could relieve the gods of their toil. At the celebration of the birth, however, Enki and Ninmah both drank too much beer and began to quarrel. Ninmah boasted that she could impair a human shape at will, and Enki countered that he could temper even the worst that she might do. So she made seven freaks, for each of which Enki found a place in society and a living. He then challenged her to alleviate the mischief he could do, but the creature he fashioned—a prematurely aborted fetus—was beyond help. The moral drawn by Enki was that both male and female contribute to the birth of a happy child. The aborted fetus lacked the contribution of the birth goddess in the womb.

The ordering, rather than the creation, of the world is the subject of another myth about Enki, called "Enki and World Order." Beginning with long praises and self-praises of Enki, it tells how he blessed Nippur (Sumer), Ur, Meluhha (coastal region of the Indian Ocean), and Dilmun (Bahrain) and gave them their characteristics, after which he turned his attention to the Euphrates and Tigris rivers, to the marshes, the sea, and the rains, and then to instituting one facet after another of the economic life of Sumer: agriculture, housebuilding, herding, and so forth. The story ends with a complaint by Enki's granddaughter Inanna that she has not been given her due share of offices, at which he patiently pointed to various offices she had in fact been given and kindly added a few more.

Another myth about the world order but dealing with it from a very different point of view concerns Enlil's son, the rain god Ninurta, called from its opening word *Lugal-e*

("O King"). This myth begins with a description of the young king, Ninurta, sitting at home in Nippur when, through his general, reports reach him of a new power that has arisen in the mountains to challenge him—i.e., Azag, son of Anu (Sky) and Ki (Earth), who has been chosen king by the plants and is raiding the cities with his warriors, the stones. Ninurta sets out in his boat to give battle, and a fierce engagement ensues, in which Azag is killed. Afterward Ninurta reorganizes his newly won territory, builds a stone barrier, the near mountain ranges or foothills (the *hursag*), and gathers the waters that used to go up into the mountains and directs them into the Tigris to flood it and provide plentiful irrigation water from Sumer. The *hursag* he presents as a gift to his mother, who had come to visit him, naming her Ninhursag (Lady of the Hursag). Lastly he sits in judgment on the stones who had formed Azag's army. Some of

A cuneiform tablet retelling the myth "Enki and the World Order." DEA/G. Dagli Orti/De Agostini/Getty Images

them, who had shown special ill will toward him, he curses, and others he trusts and gives high office in his administration. These judgments give the stones their present characteristics so that, for example, the flint is condemned to break before the much softer horn, as it indeed does when the horn is pressed against it to flake it. Noteworthy also is the way in which order in the universe, the yearly flood and other seasonal events, is seen—consonantly with Ninurta's role as "king" and leader in war—under the pattern of a reorganization of conquered territories.

Other myths about Ninurta are *An-gim dím-ma* and a myth of his contest with Enki. The first of these tells how Ninurta, on returning from battle to Nippur, was met by Enlil's page Nusku, who ordered him to cease his warlike clamour and not scare Enlil and the other gods. After long speeches of self-praise by Ninurta, further addresses to him calmed him and made him enter his temple gently. The second tale relates how he conquered the Thunderbird Anzu with Enki's help but missed the powers it had stolen from him, and how, resentful at this, he plotted against Enki but was outsmarted and trapped. Another Sumerian myth, the "Eridu Genesis," tells of the creation of humanity and of animals, of the building of the first cities, and of the Flood.

CHAPTER 1

THE HISTORY AND LITERATURE OF MESOPOTAMIA

Human occupation of Mesopotamia—"the land between the rivers" (i.e., the Tigris and Euphrates)— seems to reach back farthest in time in the north (Assyria), where the earliest settlers built their small villages some time around 6000 BCE. The prehistoric cultural stages of Ḥassūna-Sāmarrāʿ and Ḥalaf (named after the sites of archaeological excavations) succeeded each other here before there is evidence of settlement in the south (the area that was later called Sumer). There the earliest settlements, such as Eridu, appear to have been founded about 5000 BCE, in the late Ḥalaf period. From then on the cultures of the north and south move through a succession of major archaeological periods that in their southern forms are known as Ubaid, Warka, and Protoliterate (during which writing was invented), at the end of which—shortly after 3000 BCE—recorded history begins. The historical periods of the 3rd millennium are, in order, Early Dynastic, Akkad, Gutium, and 3rd dynasty of Ur; those of the 2nd millennium are Isin-Larsa, Old Babylonian, Kassite, and Middle Babylonian; and those of the 1st millennium are Assyrian, Neo-Babylonian, Achaemenian, Seleucid, and Parthian.

Politically, an early division of the country into small independent city-states, loosely organized in a league with the centre in Nippur, was followed by a unification by force under King Lugalzagesi (c. 2375–2350 BCE) of Uruk, just before the Akkadian period. The unification was maintained by his successors, the kings of Akkad, who built it into an empire, and—after a brief interruption by Gutian invaders—by Utu-hegal (c. 2116–c. 2110 BCE) of Uruk and the rulers of the 3rd dynasty of Ur (c. 2112–c. 2004 BCE). When Ur fell, about 2000 BCE, the country again divided into smaller units, with the cities Isin and Larsa vying for hegemony. Eventually Babylon established a lasting national state in the south, while Ashur dominated a similar rival state, Assyria, in the north. From the 1st millennium BCE onward, Assyria built an empire comprising, for a short time, all of the ancient Middle East. This political and administrative achievement remained essentially intact under the following Neo-Babylonian and Persian kings down to the conquests of Alexander the Great (331 BCE).

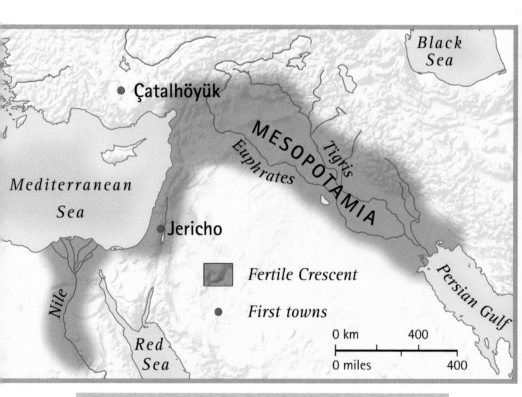

Map of the Fertile Crescent of Mesopotamia and Egypt and the location of first towns. Dorling Kindersley RF/Thinkstock

Stages of Religious Development

The religious development—as indeed that of the Mesopotamian culture generally—was not significantly influenced by the movements of the various

Third-millennium BCE Sumerian clay tablet with cuneiform script. DEA/G. Dagli Orti/De Agostini/Getty Images

peoples into and within the area—the Sumerians, Akkadians, Gutians, Kassites, Hurrians, Aramaeans, and Chaldeans. Rather it forms a uniform, consistent, and coherent Mesopotamian tradition changing in response to its own internal needs of insights and expression. It is possible to discern a basic substratum involving worship of the forces in nature—often visualized in nonhuman forms—especially those that were of immediate import to basic economic pursuits. Many of these figures belong to the type of the "dying god" (a fertility deity displaying death and regeneration characteristics) but show variant traits according to whether they are powers of fertility worshipped by marsh dwellers, orchard growers, herders, or farmers. This stage may be tentatively dated back to the 4th millennium BCE and even earlier. A second stage, characterized by a visualization of the gods as human in shape and organized in a polity of a primitive democratic cast in which each deity had his or her special offices and functions, overlaid and conditioned the religious forms and characteristics of the earlier stage during the 3rd millennium BCE. Lastly, a third stage evolved during the 2nd and 1st millennia BCE. It was characterized by a growing emphasis on personal religion involving concepts of sin and forgiveness and by a change of the earlier democratic divine polity into an absolute monarchical structure, dominated by the god of the national state—to the point that the pious abstained from all human initiative, in absolute faith and reliance on divine intervention. As a result of this development, since the ancient Mesopotamians were intensely conservative in religious matters and unwilling to discard anything of a hallowed past, the religious data of any period, and particularly that of the later periods, is a condensed version of earlier millennia that must be carefully analyzed and placed in proper perspective before it can be evaluated.

THE LITERARY LEGACY: MYTH AND EPIC

Present knowledge of ancient Mesopotamian religion rests almost exclusively on archaeological evidence recovered from the ruined city-mounds of Mesopotamia since the 19th century. Of greatest significance is the literary evidence, texts written in cuneiform (wedge-shaped) script on tablets made of clay or, for monumental purposes, on stone. Central, of course, are the specifically religious texts comprising god lists, myths, hymns, laments, prayers, rituals, omen texts, incantations, and other forms; however, since religion permeated the culture, giving form and meaning to all aspects of it, any written text, any work of art, or any of its material remains are directly or indirectly related to the religion and may further scholarly knowledge of it.

Among the archaeological finds that have particularly helped to throw light on religion are the important discoveries of inscribed tablets with Sumerian texts in copies of Old Babylonian date (c.1800–c. 1600 BCE) at Nippur and Ur, the Sumerian and Akkadian texts of the 2nd and 1st millennia from Ashur and Sultantepe, and particularly the all-important library of the Assyrian king Ashurbanipal (reigned 668–627 BCE) from Nineveh. Of nonliterary remains, the great temples and temple towers (ziggurats) excavated at almost all major sites— e.g., Eridu, Ur, Nippur, Babylon, Ashur, Kalakh (biblical Calah), Nineveh—as well as numerous works of art from various periods, are important sources of information.

The Uruk Vase, with its representation of the rite of the sacred marriage, the Naram-Sin stela (inscribed commemorative pillar), the Ur-Nammu stela, and the stela with the Code of Hammurabi (Babylonian king, 18th century BCE), which shows at its top the royal lawgiver before the sun god Shamash, the divine guardian of justice, are important works of art that may be singled out. Other important sources are the representations on cylinder seals and on boundary stones (*kudurrus*), both of

Eighteenth-century BCE *diorite stela, or stone slab, bearing the Code of Hammurabi.* DEA/G. Dagli Orti/De Agostini/Getty Images

which provide rich materials for religious iconography in certain periods.

In working with, and seeking to interpret, these varied sources, two difficulties stand out: the incompleteness of the data and the remoteness of the ancients from modern people, not only in time but also in experience and in ways of thought. Thus, for all periods before the 3rd millennium, scholars must rely on scarce, nonliterary data only, and, even though writing appears shortly before that millennium, it is only in its latter half that written data become numerous enough and readily understandable enough to be of significant help. It is generally necessary, therefore, to interpret the scarce data of the older periods in the light of survivals and of what is known from later periods, an undertaking that calls for critical acumen if anachronisms are to be avoided. Also, for the later periods, the evidence flows unevenly, with perhaps the middle of the 2nd millennium BCE the least well-documented and hence least-known age.

As for the difficulties raised by differences in the ways of thinking between modern people and the ancients, they are of the kind that one always meets in trying to understand something unfamiliar and strange. A contemporary inquirer must keep his accustomed values and modes of thought in suspension and seek rather the inner coherence and structure of the data with which he deals, in order to enter sympathetically into the world out of which they came, just as one does, for example, in entering the sometimes intensely private world of a poem, or, on a slightly different level, in learning the new, unexpected meanings and overtones of the words and phrases of a foreign language.

SUMERIAN LITERATURE

Mesopotamian literature originated with the Sumerians, whose earliest known written records are from the middle of the 4th millennium BCE. It constitutes the oldest known literature in the world; moreover, inner criteria indicate that a long oral-literary tradition preceded, and probably coexisted with, the setting down of its songs and stories in writing. It may be assumed, further, that this oral literature developed the genres of the core literature. The handbook genres, however, in spite of occasional inclusions of oral formula—e.g., legal or medical—may generally be assumed to have been devised after writing had been invented, as a response to the remarkable possibilities that writing offered for amassing and organizing data.

The purpose underlying the core literature and its oral prototypes would seem to have been as much magical as aesthetic, or merely entertaining, in origin. In magic, words create and call into being what they state. The more vivid and expressive the words are, the more they are believed to be efficacious—so by its expressiveness literature forms a natural vehicle of such creativity. In ancient Mesopotamia its main purpose appears to have been the enhancement of what was seen as beneficial. With the sole exception of wisdom literature, the core genres are panegyric in nature (i.e., they praise something or someone), and the magical power and use of praise is to instill, call up, or activate the virtues presented in the praise.

That praise is of the essence of hymns, for instance, is shown by the fact that over and over again the encomiast, the official praiser, whose task it was to sing these hymns, closed with the standing phrase: "O [the name of a deity or human hero], thy praise is sweet." The same phrase is common also at the end of myths and epics, two further praise genres that also belonged in the repertoire of the encomiast. They praise not only in description but also in narrative, by recounting acts of valour done by the hero, thus sustaining and enhancing his power to do such deeds, according to the magical view.

In time, possibly quite early, the magical aspect of literature must have tended to fade from consciousness, yielding to more nearly aesthetic attitudes that viewed the praise hymns as expressions of allegiance and loyalty and accepted the narrative genres of myth and epic for the enjoyment of the story and the values expressed, poetic and otherwise.

Hymns, myths, and epics all were believed to sustain existing powers and virtues by means of praise, but laments were understood to praise blessings and powers lost, originally seeking to hold on to and recall them magically, through the power in the expression of intense longing for them and the vivid representation of them. The lamentation genre was the province of a separate professional, the elegist. It contained dirges for the dying gods of the fertility cults and laments for temples and cities that had been destroyed and desecrated. The laments for temples—which, as far as is known, go back no earlier than to the 3rd dynasty of Ur—were used to recall the beauties of the lost temple as a kind of inducement to persuade the god and the owner of the temple to restore it.

Penitential psalms lament private illnesses and misfortunes and seek to evoke the pity of the deity addressed and thus to gain divine aid. The genre apparently is late in date, most likely Old Babylonian (c. 19th century BCE), and in it the element of magic has, to all intents and purposes, disappeared.

The core genres of Mesopotamian literature were developed by the Sumerians apparently as oral compositions. Writing, which is first attested at the middle of the 4th millennium BCE, was in its origins predominantly logographic (i.e., each word or morpheme was represented by a single graph or symbol) and long remained a highly imperfect means of rendering the spoken word. Even as late as the beginning of the Early Dynastic III period in southern Mesopotamia, in the early 3rd millennium BCE, the preserved written literary texts have the character of mnemonic (memory) aids only and seem to presuppose that the reader has prior knowledge of the text.

As writing developed more and more precision during the 3rd millennium BCE, more oral compositions seem to have been put into writing. With the 3rd dynasty of Ur a considerable body of literature had come into being and was being added to by a generation of highly gifted authors. Fortunately for its survival, this literature became part of the curriculum in the Sumerian scribal schools. It was studied and copied by student after student so that an abundance of copies, reaching a peak in Old Babylonian times, duplicated and supplemented each other as witnesses to the text of the major works. Fifty or more copies or fragments of copies of a single composition may support a modern edition, and many thousands more copies probably lie unread, still buried in the earth.

EPICS

The genre of epics appears generally to be younger in origin than that of myths and apparently was linked—in subject matter and values—to the emergence of monarchy at the middle of the Early Dynastic period. The works that have survived seem, however, all to be of later date. A single short Sumerian epic tale, "Gilgamesh and Agga of Kish," is told in the style of primary epic. It deals with

Gilgamesh's successful rebellion against his overlord and former benefactor, Agga of Kish. More in the style of romantic epic are the stories of "Enmerkar and the Lord of Aratta," "Enmerkar and Ensuhkeshdanna," and the "Lugalbanda Epic," all of which have as heroes rulers of the 1st dynasty of Uruk (c. 2500 BCE) and deal with wars between that city and the fabulous city of Aratta in the eastern highlands. Gilgamesh, also of that dynasty, figures as the hero of a variety of short tales; some, such as "Gilgamesh and Huwawa" and "Gilgamesh and the Bull of Heaven," are in romantic epic style, and others, such as "The Death of Gilgamesh" and "Gilgamesh, Enkidu, and the Netherworld," concern the inescapable fact of death and the character of afterlife.

Akkadian Literature

The first centuries of the 2nd millennium BCE witnessed the demise of Sumerian as a spoken language and its replacement by Akkadian. However, Sumerian (much as Latin in the Middle Ages) continued to be taught and spoken in the scribal schools throughout the 2nd and 1st millennia BCE because of its role as bearer of Sumerian culture, as the language of religion, literature, and many arts. New compositions were even composed in Sumerian. As time passed these grew more and more corrupt in grammar.

Akkadian, when it supplanted Sumerian as the spoken language of Mesopotamia, was not without its own literary tradition. Writing, to judge from Akkadian orthographic peculiarities, was very early borrowed from the Sumerians. By Old Babylonian times (c.19th century BCE), the literature in Akkadian, partly under the influence of Sumerian models and Sumerian literary themes, had developed myths and epics of its own, among them the superb Old Babylonian Gilgamesh epic as well as hymns, disputation texts (evaluations of elements of the cosmos and society), penitential psalms, and not a few independent new handbook genres—e.g., omens, rituals, laws and legal phrasebooks (often translated from Sumerian), mathematical texts, and grammatical texts. There was a significant amount of translation from Sumerian; translations include incantation series such as the *Utukki lemnuti* ("The Evil Spirits"), laments for destroyed temples, penitential psalms, and others. The prestige of Sumerian as a literary language, however, is indicated by the fact that translations were rarely, if ever, allowed to supersede the original Sumerian text. The Sumerian text was kept with an interlinear translation to form a bilingual work.

Fourteenth-century BCE *clay fragment displaying script in the Akkadian language, the oldest written document ever found in Jerusalem.* Getty Images

The continued study and copying of literature in the schools, both Sumerian and Akkadian, by the middle of the 2nd millennium led to a remarkable effort of standardizing, or canonizing. Texts of the same genre were collected, often under royal auspices and with royal support, and were then sifted and finally edited in series that henceforth were recognized as the canonical form. Authoritative texts were established for incantations, laments, omens, medical texts, lexical texts, and others. In myths and epics, such major and lengthy compositions as the Akkadian creation story *Enuma elish*, the Erra myth, the myth of Nergal and Ereshkigal, the Etana legend, the Gilgamesh epic, and the Tukulti-Ninurta epic were reworked or re-created.

Of special interest are philosophical compositions, such as the Akkadian *Ludlul bel nemeqi*, "Let Me Praise the Lord of Wisdom," and theodicies (justification of divine ways) that deal with the problem of the just sufferer, similar to the biblical Job. They constitute a high point in the genre of wisdom literature. From the 1st millennium BCE the rise of factual historical chronicles and a spate of political and religious polemical writings reflecting the rivalry between Assyria and Babylonia deserve mention. Very late in the millennium, the first astronomical texts appeared.

MYTHS

The Akkadian myths are in many ways dependent on Sumerian materials, but they show an originality and a broader scope in their treatment of the earlier Sumerian concepts and forms; they address themselves more often to existence as a whole. Fairly close to Sumerian prototypes is an Akkadian version of the myth of "Inanna's Descent." An Old Babylonian myth about the Thunderbird Anzu, who stole the tablets of fates and was conquered by Ninurta, who was guided by Enki's counsel, is probably closely related to the Sumerian story of Ninurta's contest with Enki.

Also important is an Old Babylonian "Myth of Atrahasis," which, in motif, shows a relationship with the account of the creation of human beings to relieve the gods of toil in the "Enki and Ninmah" myth, and with

Third-century BCE *cylinder seal illustrating Ea, the Mesopotamian god of water, with streams flowing from his body.* Werner Forman/Universal Images Group/Getty Images

a Sumerian account of the Flood in the "Eridu Genesis." The Atrahasis myth, however, treats these themes with noticeable originality and remarkable depth. It relates, first, how the gods originally had to toil for a living, how they rebelled and went on strike, how Enki suggested that one of their number—the god We, apparently the ringleader who "had the idea"—be killed and humankind created from clay mixed with his flesh and blood, so that the toil of the gods could be laid on humankind and the gods left to go free. But after Enki and the birth goddess Nintur (another name for Ninmah) had created humans, they multiplied at such a rate that the din they made kept Enlil sleepless. At first Enlil had Namtar, the god of death, cause a plague to diminish the human population, but the wise Atrahasis, at the advice of Enki, had human beings concentrate all worship and offerings on Namtar. Namtar, embarrassed at hurting people who showed such love and affection for him, stayed his hand. Next Enlil had Adad, the god of rains, hold back the rains and thus cause a famine, but, because of the same stratagem, Adad was embarrassed and released the rains. After this, Enlil planned a famine by divine group action that would not be vulnerable as the earlier actions by individual gods had been. Anu and Adad were to guard the heavens, Enlil himself earth, and Enki the waters underground and the sea so that no gift of nature could come through to the human race. The ensuing famine was terrible. By the seventh year one house consumed the other and people began eating their own children. At that point Enki—accidentally he maintained—let through a wealth of fish from the sea and so the humans were saved. With this, however, Enlil's patience was at an end and he thought of the Flood as a means to get rid of humanity once and for all. Enki, however, warned Atrahasis and had him build a boat in which he saved himself, his family, and all animals. After the Flood had abated and the ship was grounded, Atrahasis sacrificed, and the hungry gods, much chastened, gathered around the offering. Only Enlil was unrelenting until Enki upbraided him for killing innocent and guilty alike and—there is a gap in the text—suggested other means to keep human numbers down. In consultation with the birth goddess Nintur, Enki then developed a scheme of birth control by inventing the barren woman, the demon Pashittu who kills children at birth, and the various classes of priestesses to whom giving birth was taboo.

The myth uses the motif of the protest of the gods against their hard toil and the creation of humans to relieve it, which was depicted earlier in the Sumerian

Limestone engraving depicting Babylonian king Nebuchadrezzar I. Album/Prisma/SuperStock

myth of "Enki and Ninmah," and also the motif of the Flood, which occurred in the "Eridu Genesis." The import of these motifs here is, however, new: they bring out the basic precariousness of human existence; mankind's usefulness to the gods will not protect them unless they take care not to annoy them, however innocently. They must stay within bounds; there are limits set for self-expression.

A far more trustful and committed attitude toward the powers that rule existence finds expression in the seemingly slightly later Babylonian creation story, *Enuma elish*, which may be dated to the later part of the 1st dynasty of Babylon (c. 1894–c. 1595 BCE). Babylon's

archenemy at that time was the Sealand, which con-
trolled Nippur and the country south of it—the ancestral
country of Sumerian civilization. This lends political
point to the battle of Marduk (thunder and rain deity),
the god of Babylon, with the sea, Tiamat; it also accounts
for the odd, almost complete silence about Enlil of
Nippur in the tale.

The myth tells how in the beginning there was noth-
ing but Apsu, the sweet waters underground, and Tiamat,
the sea, mingling their waters together. In these waters
the first gods came into being, and generation followed
generation. The gods represented energy and activity and
thus differed markedly from Apsu and Tiamat, who stood
for rest and inertia. True to their nature, the gods gathered to dance, and in so doing, surging back and forth,
they disturbed the insides of Tiamat. Finally, Apsu's
patience was at an end, and he thought of doing away
with the gods, but Tiamat, as a true mother, demurred at
destroying her own offspring. Apsu, however, did not
swerve from his decision, and he was encouraged in this
by his page Mummu, "the original (watery) form." When
the youngest of the gods, the clever Ea (Sumerian: Enki),
heard about the planned attack he forestalled it by means
of a powerful spell with which he poured slumber on
Apsu, killed him, and built his temple over him. He seized
Mummu and held him captive by a nose rope.

In the temple thus built the hero of the myth,
Marduk, was born. From the first he was the darling of
his grandfather, the god of heaven, Anu, who engendered
the four winds for him to play with. As they blew and
churned up waves, the disturbing of Tiamat—and of a
faction of the gods who shared her desire for rest—
became more and more unbearable. At last these gods
succeeded in rousing her to resistance, and she created a
mighty army with a spearhead of monsters to destroy

Babylonian seal depicting the moon god Sin, facing left, standing on a crescent and receiving a prayer by the man standing before him. Facing right another man prays before a sirrush, *a creature symbolizing Marduk.* Werner Forman/Universal Images Group/Getty Images

the gods. She placed her consort Kingu at the head of it and gave him absolute powers.

When news of these developments reached the gods there was consternation. Ea was sent to make Tiamat desist, and then Anu, but to no avail. Finally Anshar, god of the horizon and king of the gods, thought of young Marduk. Marduk proved willing to fight Tiamat but demanded absolute authority. Accordingly, a messenger was sent to the oldest of the gods, Lahmu and Lahamu, to call the gods to assembly. In the assembly the gods conferred absolute authority on Marduk, tested it by seeing whether his word of command alone could destroy a constellation and then again make it whole, hailed him king, and set him on the road of "security and obedience," a formula of allegiance that based his power and authority on the pressing need for protection of the moment.

In the ensuing encounter with Tiamat's forces Kingu and his army lost heart when they saw Marduk. Only Tiamat stood her ground, seeking first to throw him off his guard by flattery about his quick rise to leadership, but Marduk angrily denounced her and the older generation: "The sons [had to] withdraw [for] the fathers were acting treacherously, and [now] you, who gave birth to them, bear malice to the offspring." At this Tiamat, furious, attacked, but Marduk loosed the winds against her, pierced her heart with an arrow, and killed her. Kingu and the gods who had sided with her he took captive.

Having thus won a lasting victory for his suzerain, King Anshar, Marduk gave thought to what he might do further. Cleaving the carcass of Tiamat, he raised half of her to form heaven, ordered the constellations, the calendar, the movements of Sun and Moon, and, keeping control of atmospheric phenomena for himself, made the Earth out of the other half of her, arranging its mountains and rivers. Having organized the various administrative tasks, he put their supervision in Ea's hands; to Anu he gave the tablets of fate he had taken from Kingu. His prisoners he paraded in triumphal procession before his fathers, and as a monument to his victory he set up images of Tiamat's monsters at the gate of his parental home. The gods were overjoyed to see him; Anshar rushed toward him and Marduk formally announced to him the state of security he had achieved. He then bathed, dressed, and seated himself on his throne, with the spear Security and Obedience, named from his mandate, at his side. By now, however, the situation had subtly altered. The old fear and urgent need for protection was gone, but in its stead had come a promise held out by Marduk's organizational powers; so when the gods reaffirmed their allegiance to him as king they used a new formula: "benefits and obedience." From then on Marduk would take care of their sanctuaries and they, in turn, would obey him.

Marduk then announced his intention of building a city for himself, Babylon, with room for the gods when they come there for assembly. His fathers suggested that they move to Babylon themselves to be with him and help in the administration of the world he had created. Next, he pardoned the gods who had sided with Tiamat and had been captured, charging them with the building tasks. Grateful for their lives, they prostrated themselves before him, hailed him as king, and promised to do the building.

Pleased with their willingness, Marduk magnanimously wanted to relieve them even from this chore and planned to create humans to do the toil for them. At the advice of his father Ea, he then had them indict Kingu as instigator of the rebellion. Kingu was duly sentenced and executed, and from his blood Ea created humankind. Then Marduk divided the gods into a celestial and a terrestrial group, assigned them their tasks in the cosmos, and allotted them their stipends. Thus freed from all burdens, the gods wanted to show their gratitude to Marduk, and as a token they took, of their own free will, for one last time, spade in hand to build Babylon and Marduk's temple, Esagila. In the new temple the gods then assembled and distributed the celestial and terrestrial offices. The "great gods" went into session and permanently appointed the "seven gods of destinies," or better "of the decrees," who would formulate in final form the decrees enacted by the assembly. Marduk then presented his weapons, and Anu adopted the bow as his daughter and gave it a seat among the gods. Lastly, Marduk was enthroned, and after the gods had prostrated themselves before him they bound themselves by oath—touching their throats with oil and water—and formally gave him kingship, appointing him permanently lord of the gods of heaven and earth. After this they solemnly listed his 50 names expressive of his power and achievements. The myth ends with a plea that it be handed on from father to son and told to future rulers, that they may heed Marduk: it is the song of Marduk who bound Tiamat and assumed the kingship.

The motifs from which this myth is built are in large measure known from elsewhere. The initial generation of the gods is a variant form of the genealogy of Anu in the great god list *An: Anum*. The threat to annihilate the disturbers of sleep are known from the Atrahasis and the Sumerian Flood traditions. The battle of Marduk with Tiamat seems to stem from western myths of a battle between the thunder god and the sea. The organization of the universe after victory recalls the organization of conquered territory in *Lugal-e*. The killing of a rebel god to create the human race to take over the gods' toil is found in the Atrahasis myth and—without the rebel aspect—in a bilingual creation myth found in Ashur. New and original, however, is the way in which they have all been grouped and made dependent on the figure of the young king. The political form of the monarchy is seen as embracing the universe; it was the prowess of a young king that overcame the forces of inertia; it was his organizational genius that created and organized all; and it is he who—like his counterpart on earth, the human king—grants benefits in return for obedience.

The high value set on the monarchy as a guarantor of security and order in the *Enuma elish* can hardly have seemed obvious in Babylonia in the first troubled years of

Assyrian rule. From this period (c. 700 BCE) comes a myth usually called the *Erra Epic*, which reads almost like a polemic against *Enuma elish*. It tells how the god of affray and indiscriminate slaughter, Erra, persuaded Marduk to turn over the rule of the world to him while Marduk was having his royal insignia cleaned, and how Erra, true to his nature, used his powers to institute indiscriminate rioting and slaughter. Royal power here stands no longer for security and order but for the opposite: license to kill and destroy.

Two other Akkadian myths may be mentioned—both probably dating from the middle of the 2nd millennium BCE—the myth of the "Dynasty of Dunnum" and the myth of "Nergal and Ereshkigal." The first of these tells of succeeding divine generations ruling in Dunnum, the son usually killing his father and marrying, sometimes his mother, sometimes his sister, until—according to a reconstruction of the broken text—more acceptable mores came into vogue with the last generation of gods, Enlil and Ninurta. This myth underlies the Greek poet Hesiod's *Theogony*. The myth of Nergal and Ereshkigal relates the unorthodox way in which the god Nergal became the husband of Ereshkigal and king of the netherworld.

Illustration of the Greek poet Hesiod. Hulton Archive/Getty Images

EPICS

The quick rise of Sargon, the founder of the dynasty of Akkad (c. 2334–c. 2154 BCE), from obscurity to fame and his victory over Lugalzagesi of Uruk form the theme of several epic tales. The sudden eclipse of the Akkadian empire long after Naram-Sin, which was wrongly attributed to that ruler's presumed pride and the gods' retaliation, is the theme of "The Fall of Akkad." Akkadian epic tradition continues and gives focus to the Sumerian tales of Gilgamesh.

The Akkadian *Epic of Gilgamesh* seems to have been composed in Old Babylonian times but was reworked by a certain Sin-leqe-unnini later in the 1st millennium BCE. It tells how Gilgamesh, the young ruler of Uruk, drives his subjects so hard that they appeal to the gods for relief. The gods create a wild man, Enkidu, who at first lives with the animals in the desert but is lured away from them and becomes Gilgamesh's friend. Together they vanquish the terrifying Huwawa, set by Enlil to guard the cedar forest in the west, and, when on their return the goddess of Uruk, Ishtar, falls in love with Gilgamesh, is jilted by him, and sends the dread "bull of heaven" to kill him, he and Enkidu manage to kill the bull. At this point, however, their fortunes change. Enlil, angered at the killing of Huwawa, causes Enkidu to fall ill and die, and Gilgamesh, inconsolable at the death of his friend and terrified at the realization that he himself must someday die, sets out to find eternal life.

After many adventures he reaches his ancestor Utnapishtim, to whom the gods have granted eternal life, but his case proves to be a unique one and so of no help to Gilgamesh. Utnapishtim was rewarded for having saved human and animal life at the time of the great Flood.

Ninth-century BCE Syrian tablet depicting Gilgamesh between two minotaur demigods holding the sun disc. DEA/G. Dagli Orti/De Agostini/ Getty Images

Eventually, just as Gilgamesh is ready to return home, he is told about a plant that rejuvenates and transforms old people into children. Gilgamesh finds it and begins his return journey. But, as the day is warm, when he passes an inviting pool he leaves his clothes and the plant on the shore and goes in for a swim. A serpent smells the plant, comes out of its hole, and eats it. Thus Gilgamesh's quest comes to naught. Eternal life is beyond human grasp. The Gilgamesh epic is perhaps the most moving work in ancient Mesopotamian literature, with its sharp contrast

Third-century BCE *Akkadian carving illustrating the legend of Etana.*
Werner Forman/Universal Images Group/Getty Images

of values: the warrior's disdain of death and danger, which informs the early parts of the epic, and the haunting fear that drives Gilgamesh in the later parts.

Other Akkadian epics that deserve to be mentioned are the *Etana Epic*, which tells how Etana, the first king, was carried up to heaven on the back of an eagle to obtain the plant of birth so that his son could be born. Also important are the epic tales about Sargon of Akkad, one of which, the birth legend, tells of his abandonment in a casket on the river by his mother—much as the Bible tells that Moses was abandoned—and his discovery by an orchardman, who raised him as his son. Another Sargon tale is "The King of Battle," which tells about conquests in Asia Minor to protect foreign trade. Naram-Sin is the central figure in another tale dealing with that king's pride and also relating the destructive invasions by barbarous foes. A late flowering of primary epic is the Assyrian *Epic of Tukulti-Ninurta* (reigned 1243–1207 BCE), which deals with that king's wars with Babylonia.

THE MESOPOTAMIAN WORLDVIEW AS EXPRESSED IN MYTH

CHAPTER 2

The more completely a given culture is embraced, the more natural will its basic tenets seem to the people involved. The most fundamental of its presuppositions are not even likely to rise into awareness and be consciously held but are tacitly taken for granted. It takes a degree of cultural decline, of the loosening of the culture's grip on thought and action, before its most basic structural lines can be recognized and, if need be, challenged. Since culture, the total pattern within which human beings live and act, is thus not likely to be conceived of consciously and as a whole until it begins to lose its obvious and natural character, it is understandable that those myths of a culture that may be termed existential—in the sense that they articulate human existence as a whole in terms of the culture and show its basic structure—are rarely encountered until comparatively late in the history of a culture. Before that occurs, it is, rather, the particular aspects and facets of existence that are apt to claim attention.

In ancient Mesopotamia the oldest known materials, the Sumerian myths, have relatively little to say about creation; scholars must, for the most part, turn to the introductions of tales and disputations to infer how things were believed to be in the beginning. Thus, a story about the hero Gilgamesh refers in its introductory lines to the times "after heaven had been moved away from earth, after earth had been separated from heaven." The same notion that heaven and earth were once close together occurs also in a bilingual Sumero-Akkadian text from Ashur about the creation of the human race. The actual act of separating them is credited to the storm god Enlil of Nippur in the introduction to a third tale that deals with the creation of the first hoe. From similar passing remarks scholars have inferred that the gods, before humanity came into being, had to labour hard at the heavy works of irrigation for agriculture and dug out the beds of the Tigris and the Euphrates.

COSMOGONY AND COSMOLOGY

Though the "Eridu Genesis" may have come close to treating existence as a whole, a true cosmogonic and cosmological myth that deals centrally with the origins, structuring, and functional principles of the cosmos does not actually appear until Old Babylonian times, when Mesopotamian culture was entering a period of doubt about the moral character of world government and even of divine power itself. Yet, the statement is a positive one, almost to the point of defiance. *Enuma elish* tells of a beginning when all was a watery chaos and only the sea, Tiamat, and the sweet waters underground, Apsu, mingled their waters together. Mummu, the personified original watery form, served as Apsu's page. In their midst the gods were born. The first pair, Lahmu and Lahamu, represented the powers in silt; the next, Anshar and Kishar, those in the horizon. They engendered the god of heaven, Anu, and he in turn the god of the flowing sweet waters, Ea.

This tradition is known in a more complete form from an ancient list of gods called *An: Anum*. There, after a different beginning, Lahmu and Lahamu give rise to Duri and Dari, "the time-cycle"; and these in turn give rise to Enshar and Ninshar, Lord and Lady Circle. Enshar and

Ninshar engender the concrete circle of the horizon, in the persons of Anshar and Kishar, probably conceived as silt deposited along the edge of the universe. Next was the horizon of the greater heaven and earth, and then—omitting an intrusive line—heaven and earth, probably conceived as two juxtaposed flat disks formed from silt deposited inward from the horizons.

Enuma elish truncates these materials and violates their inner logic considerably. Though they are clearly cosmogonic and assume that the cosmic elements and the powers informing them come into being together, *Enuma elish* seeks to utilize them for a pure theogony (account of the origin of the gods). The creation of the actual cosmos is dealt with much later. Also, the introduction of Mummu, the personified "original form," which in the circumstances can only be that of water, may have led to the omission of Ki, Earth, who—as nonwatery—did not fit in.

The gods, who in *Enuma elish* come into being within Apsu and Tiamat, are viewed as dynamic creatures, who contrast strikingly with the older generation. Apsu and Tiamat stand for inertia and rest. This contrast leads to a series of conflicts in which first Apsu is killed by Ea; then Tiamat, who was roused later to attack the gods, is killed by Ea's son Marduk. It is Marduk, the hero of the story, who creates the extant universe out of the body of Tiamat. He cuts her, like a dried fish, in two, making one-half of her into heaven—appointing there Sun, Moon, and stars to execute their prescribed motions—and the other half into the Earth. He pierces her eyes to let the Tigris and Euphrates flow forth, and then, heaping mountains on her body in the east, he makes the various tributaries of the Tigris flow out from her breasts. The remainder of the story deals with Marduk's organization of the cosmos, his creation of human beings, and his assigning to

Depiction of Marduk defeating Tiamat, circa 2000 BCE. Pantheon/SuperStock

the gods their various cosmic offices and tasks. The cosmos is viewed as structured as, and functioning as, a benevolent absolute monarchy.

THE GODS AND DEMONS

The gods were, as mentioned previously, organized in a polity of a primitive democratic cast. They constituted, as it were, a landed nobility, each god owning and working an estate—his temple and its lands—and controlling the city in which it was located. On the national level they attended the general assembly of the gods, which was the highest authority in the cosmos, to vote on matters of national import such as election or deposition of kings. The major gods also served on the national level as officers having charge of cosmic offices. Thus, for example, Utu (Akkadian: Shamash), the sun god, was the judge of the gods, in charge of justice and righteousness generally.

Highest in the pantheon—and presiding in the divine assembly—ranked An (Akkadian: Anu), god of heaven, who was responsible for the calendar and the seasons as they were indicated by their appropriate stars. Next came Enlil of Nippur, god of winds and of agriculture, creator of the hoe. Enlil executed the verdicts of the divine assembly. Equal in rank to An and Enlil was the goddess Ninhursag (also known as Nintur and Ninmah), goddess of stony ground: the near mountain ranges in the east and the stony desert in the west with its wildlife—wild asses, gazelles, wild goats, etc. She was also the goddess of birth. With these was joined—seemingly secondarily—Enki (Ea), god of the sweet waters of rivers and marshes; he was the cleverest of the gods and a great troubleshooter, often appealed to by both gods and men. Enlil's sons were the moon god Nanna (Sin); the god of thunderstorms, floods, and the plough, Ninurta; and the underworld figures Meslamtaea, Ninazu, and Ennugi. Sin's sons were the sun god and judge of the gods, Utu; the rain god Ishkur (Akkadian: Adad); and his daughter, the goddess of war, love, and morning and evening star, Inanna (Akkadian: Ishtar). Inanna's ill-fated young husband was the herder god Dumuzi (Akkadian: Tammuz). The dread netherworld was ruled by the goddess Ereshkigal and her husband Nergal, a figure closely related to Meslamtaea and Ninurta. Earlier tradition mentions Ninazu as her husband.

Demons played little or no role in the myths or lists of the Mesopotamian pantheon. Their domain was that of incantations. Mostly, they were depicted as outlaws; the demoness Lamashtu, for instance, was hurled from heaven by her father An because of her wickedness. The demons attacked human beings by causing all kinds of diseases and were, as a rule, viewed as wind and storm beings. Consonant with the classical view of the universe as a cosmic state, it was possible for a person to go to the law courts against the demons—i.e., to seek recourse before Utu and obtain judgments against them. Various rituals for such procedures are known.

Human Origin

Two different notions about human origin seem to have been current in ancient Mesopotamian religions. Brief mentions in Sumerian texts indicate that the first human beings grew from the earth in the manner of grass and herbs. One of these texts, the "Myth of the Creation of the Hoe," adds a few details: Enlil removed heaven from earth in order to make room for seeds to come up, and after he had created the hoe he used it to break the hard crust of earth in Uzumua ("the flesh-grower"), a place in the Temple of Inanna in Nippur. Here, out of the hole made by Enlil's hoe, people grew forth.

The other notion presented the view that humankind was created from select "ingredients" by Enki, or by Enki and his mother Nammu, or by Enki and the birth goddess called variously Ninhursag, Nintur, and Ninmah. In the myth of "Enki and Ninmah" recounted above, Enki had humans sired by the "engendering clay of the Apsu"—i.e., of the waters underground—and borne by Nammu. The Akkadian tradition, as represented by the "Myth of Atrahasis," had Enki advise that a god—presumably a rebel—be killed and that the birth goddess Nintur mix his flesh and blood with clay. This was done, after which 14 womb goddesses gestated the mixture and gave birth to seven human pairs. A similar—probably derived—form of this motif is found in *Enuma elish*, in which Enki (Ea) alone fashioned humanity out of the blood of the slain rebel leader Kingu. The creation of the human race from the blood shed by two slain gods is yet another version of the motif that appears in a bilingual myth from Ashur.

Human nature, then, is part clay (earthly) and part god (divine). The divine aspect, however, is not that of a living god but rather that of a slain, powerless divinity. The Atrahasis story relates that the *etemmu* (ghost) of the slain god was left in human flesh and thus became part of human beings. It is this originally divine part of humanity, the *etemmu*, that was believed to survive at his death and to give him a shadowy afterlife in the nether-world. No other trace of a notion of divine essence in humankind is discernible; in fact, human beings were viewed as being utterly powerless to act effectively or to succeed in anything. For anything they might wish to do or achieve, they needed the help of a personal god or goddess, some deity in the pantheon who for one reason or other had taken an interest in them and helped and protected them, for "Without his personal god a man eats not."

About human destiny all sources agree. However they may have come into being, human beings were meant to toil in order to provide food, clothing, housing, and ser-vice for the gods, so that they, relieved of all manual labour, could live the life of a governing upper class, a landed nobility. In the scheme of existence humanity was thus never an end, always just a means.

A religious development covering four millennia such as one finds in ancient Mesopotamia is obviously of inter-est in and of itself. The tendencies that lead from a central concern with salvation from famine to a concern with sal-vation from attack, and finally to salvation from a sense of personal guilt, with the attendant deepening and enriching of the concept of the divine, invite close study. So also do the many moving and profound expressions of religious faith in the hymns, laments, and prayers of these religions. As one of the earliest religious systems in history to structure, and be itself structured by, the complexities of a high civilization, Mesopotamian religions are of significant interest to historians, historians of religion, and theologians. As a source from which religious insights, attitudes, and problems flowed into all of Western tradition, Mesopotamian religions are of lasting and great interest beyond themselves.

Gods and Goddesses

CHAPTER 3

ADAD

A dad was the weather god of the Babylonian and Assyrian pantheon. The name Adad may have been brought into Mesopotamia toward the end of the 3rd millennium BCE by Western (Amorite) Semites. His Sumerian equivalent was Ishkur and the West Semitic was Hadad.

Adad had a twofold aspect, being both the giver and the destroyer of life. His rains caused the land to bear grain and other food for his friends; hence his title Lord of Abundance. His storms and hurricanes, evidences of his anger against his foes, brought darkness, want, and death. Adad's father was the heaven god Anu, but he is also designated as the son of Bel, Lord of All Lands and god of the atmosphere. His consort was Shalash, which may be a Hurrian name.

The symbol of Adad was the cypress, and six was his sacred number. The bull and the lion were sacred to him. In Babylonia, Assyria, and Aleppo in Syria, he was also the god of oracles and divination. Unlike the greater gods, Adad quite possibly had no cult centre particular to himself, although he was worshiped in many of the important cities and towns of Mesopotamia, including Babylon and Ashur, the capital of Assyria.

ANSHAR AND KISHAR

Anshar and Kishar in Mesopotamian mythology, were the male and female principles the twin horizons of sky and earth. Their parents were either Apsu (the watery deep beneath the earth) and Tiamat (the personification of salt water) or Lahmu and Lahamu, the first set of twins born to Apsu and Tiamat. Anshar and Kishar, in turn, were the parents of Anu (An), the supreme heaven god.

ANU

Anu was the Mesopotamian sky god and a member of
the triad of deities completed by Enlil and Ea (Enki).
Like most sky gods, Anu, although theoretically the highest god, played only a small role in the mythology, hymns,
and cults of Mesopotamia. He was the father not only of
all the gods but also of evil spirits and demons, most
prominently the demoness Lamashtu, who preyed on
infants. Anu was also the god of kings and of the yearly
calendar. He was typically depicted in a headdress with
horns, a sign of strength.

His Sumerian counterpart, An, dates from the oldest
Sumerian period, at least 3000 BCE. Originally he seems
to have been envisaged as a great bull, a form later disassociated from the god as a separate mythological entity,
the Bull of Heaven, which was owned by An. His holy city
was Uruk (Erech), in the southern herding region, and the
bovine imagery suggests that he belonged originally to
the herders' pantheon. In Akkadian myth Anu was
assigned a consort, Antum (Antu), but she seems often to
have been confused with Ishtar (Inanna), the celebrated
goddess of love.

MESOPOTAMIAN CITY-STATES

In early dynastic times, probably as far back as historians can trace its history, Mesopotamia was divided into small units, the so-called city-states, consisting of a major city with its surrounding lands. The ruler of the city—usually entitled *ensi*—was also in charge of the temple of the city god. The spouse of the *ensi* had charge of the temple of the city goddess, and the children of the *ensi* administered the temples of the deities who were regarded as children of the city god and the city goddesses. After the foundation of larger political units, such as leagues or empires, contributions were made to a central temple of the political unit, such as the temple of Enlil at Nippur in the Nippur league. On the other hand, however, the king or other central ruler might also contribute to the shrines of local cults. When, in the 2nd and 1st millennia BCE, Babylonia and Assyria emerged as national states, their kings had responsibility for the national cult, and each monarch supervised the administration of all temples in his domain.

Archaeological site of the city-state of Uruk. Essam Al-Sudani/AFP/ Getty Images

ARINNITTI

Arinnitti (Hattian: Wurusemu) was the Hittite sun goddess, the principal deity and patron of the Hittite empire and monarchy. Her consort, the weather god Taru, was second to Arinnitti in importance, indicating that she probably originated in matriarchal times. Arinnitti's precursor seems to have been a mother-goddess of Anatolia, symbolic of earth and fertility. Arinnitti's attributes were righteous judgment, mercy, and royal authority. The powerful Hittite queen Puduhepa adopted Arinnitti as her protectress; the queen's seal showed her in the goddess's embrace.

ASALLUHE

A salluhe was a Sumerian deity, city god of Ku'ara, near Eridu in the southern marshland region. Asalluhe was active with the god Enki (Akkadian: Ea) in rituals of lustration (purification) magic and was considered his son. He may have originally been a god of thundershowers and would thus have corresponded to the other Sumerian gods Ishkur and Ninurta. In incantations Asalluhe was usually the god who first called Enki's attention to existing evils. He was later identified with Marduk of Babylon.

ASHUR

A shur was the city god of Ashur and national god of Assyria. In the beginning he was perhaps only a local deity of the city that shared his name. From about 1800 BCE onward, however, there appear to have been strong tendencies to identify him with the Sumerian Enlil (Akkadian: Bel), while under the Assyrian king Sargon II (reigned 721–705 BCE), there were tendencies to identify Ashur with Anshar, the father of An (Akkadian: Anu) in the creation myth. Under Sargon's successor Sennacherib, deliberate and thorough attempts were made to transfer to Ashur the primeval achievements of Marduk, as well as the whole ritual of the New Year festival of Babylon— attempts that clearly have their background in the political struggle going on at that time between Babylonia and Assyria. As a consequence, the image of Ashur seems to lack all real distinctiveness and contains little that is not implied in his position as the city god of a vigorous and warlike city that became the capital of an empire. The Assyrians believed that he granted rule over Assyria and supported Assyrian arms against enemies; detailed written reports from the Assyrian kings about their campaigns were even submitted to him. He appears a mere personification of the interests of Assyria as a political entity, with little character of his own.

DAGAN

Dagan, also spelled Dagon, was the West Semitic god of crop fertility, worshiped extensively throughout the ancient Middle East. Dagan was the Hebrew and Ugaritic common noun for "grain," and the god Dagan was the legendary inventor of the plow. His cult is attested as early as about 2500 BCE, and, according to texts found at Ras Shamra (ancient Ugarit), he was the father of the god Baal. Dagan had an important temple at Ras Shamra, and in Palestine, where he was particularly known as a god of the Philistines. He had several sanctuaries, including those at Beth-dagon in Asher (Joshua 19:27), Gaza (Judges 16:23), and Ashdod (1 Samuel 5:2–7). At Ras Shamra, Dagan was apparently second in importance only to El, the supreme god, although his functions as a god of vegetation seem to have been transferred to Baal by about 1500 BCE.

DAMU

amu, a Sumerian deity, was the city god of Girsu, east of Ur in the southern orchards region. Damu, son of Enki, was a vegetation god, especially of the vernal flowing of the sap of trees and plants. His name means "The Child," and his cult—apparently celebrated primarily by women—centred on the lamentation and search for Damu, who had lain under the bark of his nurse, the cedar tree, and had disappeared. The search finally ended when the god reappeared out of the river.

The cult of Damu influenced and later blended with the similar cult of Tammuz the Shepherd, a Sumerian deity. A different deity called Damu was a goddess of healing and the daughter of Nininsina of Isin.

DUMUZI-ABZU

The Sumerian deity Dumuzi-Abzu was the city goddess of Kinirsha near Lagash in the southeastern marshland region. She represented the power of fertility and new life in the marshes. Dumuzi-Abzu corresponded to the Sumerian god Dumuzi of the central steppe area, and thus around Eridu she was viewed as male and as son of Enki (Akkadian: Ea, also called the Lord of Apsu).

ENKI

Enki (Akkadian: Ea) was the Mesopotamian god of water and a member of the triad of deities completed by Anu (Sumerian: An) and Enlil. From a local deity worshiped in the city of Eridu, Enki evolved into a major god, Lord of Apsu (also spelled Abzu), the fresh waters beneath the earth (although Enki means literally "lord of the earth"). In the Sumerian myth "Enki and the World Order," Enki is said to have fixed national boundaries and assigned gods their roles. According to another Sumerian myth Enki is the creator, having devised men as slaves to the gods. In his original form, as Enki, he was associated with semen and amniotic fluid, and therefore with fertility. He was commonly represented as a half-goat, half-fish creature, from which the modern astrological figure for Capricorn is derived.

Third-millennium BCE depiction of Enki. Iberfoto/SuperStock

CULTIC PRACTICES

In the cultic practices of Mesopotamia, humans fulfilled their destiny: to take care of the gods' material needs. They therefore provided the gods with houses (the temples) that were richly supplied with lands, which people cultivated for them. In the temple the god was present in—but not bounded by—a statue made of precious wood overlaid with gold. For this statue the temple kitchen staff prepared daily meals from victuals grown or raised on the temple's fields, in its orchards, in its sheepfolds, cattle pens, and game preserves, brought in by its fishermen, or delivered by farmers owing it as a temple tax. The statue was also clad in costly raiment, bathed, and escorted to bed in the bedchamber of the god, often on top of the temple tower, or ziggurat. To see to all of this the god had a corps of house servants—i.e., priests trained as cooks, bakers, waiters, and bathers, or as encomiasts (singers of praise) and musicians to make the god's meals festive, or as elegists to soothe him in times of stress and grief. Diversions from the daily routine were the great monthly festivals and also a number of special occasions. Such special occasions might be a sudden need to go through the elaborate ritual for purifying the king when he was threatened by the evils implied in an eclipse of the

Model of ancient Babylonian temple, or ziggurat. Dorling Kindersley/ Getty Images

Moon, or in extreme cases there might be a call for the ritual instal-lation of a substitute king to take upon himself the dangers threatening, and various other nonperiodic rituals.

Partly regular, partly impromptu, were the occasions for audi-ences with the god in which the king or other worshippers presented their petitions and prayers accompanied by appropriate offerings. These were mostly edibles, but not infrequently the costly containers in which they were presented, stone vases, golden boat-shaped ves-sels, etc., testified to the ardour of the givers. Appropriate gifts other than edibles were also acceptable—among them cylinder seals for the god's use, superhuman in size, and weapons for him, such as mace-heads, also outsize.

To the cult, but as private rather than as part of the temple cult, may be counted also the burial ritual, concerning which, unfortu-nately, little is known. In outgoing Early Dynastic times in Girsu two modes of burial were current. One was ordinary burial in a cemetery; the nature of the other, called laying the body "in the reeds of Enki," is not understood. It may have denoted the floating of the body down the river into the canebrakes. Elegists and other funerary personnel were in attendance and conducted the laments seeking to give full expression to the grief of the bereaved and propitiate the spirit of the dead. In later times burial in a family vault under the dwelling house was frequent.

Ea, the Akkadian counterpart of Enki, was the god of ritual purification: ritual cleansing waters were called "Ea's water." Ea governed the arts of sorcery and incanta-tion. In some stories he was also the form-giving god, and thus the patron of craftsmen and artists; he was known as the bearer of culture. In his role as adviser to the king, Ea was a wise god although not a forceful one. In Akkadian myth, as Ea's character evolves, he appears frequently as a clever mediator who could be devious and cunning. He is also significant in Akkadian mythology as the father of Marduk, the national god of Babylonia.

ENLIL

Enlil was the Mesopotamian god of the atmosphere and a member of the triad of gods completed by Anu (Sumerian: An) and Ea (Enki). Enlil meant Lord Wind: both the hurricane and the gentle winds of spring were thought of as the breath issuing from his mouth and eventually as his word or command. He was sometimes called Lord of the Air.

Although An was the highest god in the Sumerian pantheon, Enlil had a more important role as the embodiment of energy and force and authority. Enlil's cult centre was Nippur. Enlil was also the god of agriculture. The "Myth of the Creation of the Hoe" describes how he separated heaven and earth to make room for seeds to grow. He then invented the hoe and broke the hard crust of earth; men sprang forth from the opening. Another myth relates Enlil's rape of his consort Ninlil (Akkadian: Belit), a grain goddess, and his subsequent banishment to the underworld. This myth reflects the agricultural cycle of fertilization, ripening, and winter inactivity.

Enlil was eventually replaced by Marduk as the executive of the Babylonian pantheon. He continued to be extolled, however, as high god of Nippur until the end of the 2nd millennium BCE. He remained an important deity there well into the next millennium.

ENMERKAR

Enmerkar was an ancient Sumerian hero and king of Uruk (Erech), a city-state in southern Mesopotamia, who is thought to have lived at the end of the 4th or beginning of the 3rd millennium BCE. Along with Lugalbanda and Gilgamesh, Enmerkar is one of the three most significant figures in the surviving Sumerian epics. Although scholars once assumed that there was only one epic relating Enmerkar's subjugation of a rival city, Aratta, it is now believed that two separate epics tell this tale. One is called *Enmerkar and the Lord of Aratta*. The longest Sumerian epic yet discovered, it is the source of important information about the history and culture of the Sumero-Iranian border area. According to this legend, Enmerkar, son of the sun god Utu, was envious of Aratta's wealth of metal and stone, which he needed in order to build various shrines, especially a temple for the god Enki in Eridu. Enmerkar therefore requested his sister, the goddess Inanna, to aid him in acquiring material and man-power from Aratta; she agreed and advised him to send a threatening message to the lord of Aratta. The lord of Aratta, however, demanded that Enmerkar first deliver large amounts of grain to him. Though Enmerkar complied, the lord of Aratta refused to complete his part of the agreement; threatening messages were again sent out by both men, each claiming the aid and sanction of the goddess Inanna. The text becomes fragmented at that point in the narrative, but in the end Enmerkar was apparently victorious.

The other epic relating the defeat of Aratta is known as *Enmerkar and Ensuhkeshdanna*. In this tale the ruler of Aratta, Ensuhkeshdanna (or Ensukushsiranna), demanded that Enmerkar become his vassal. Enmerkar refused and, declaring himself the favourite of the gods, commanded Ensuhkeshdanna to submit to him. Although the members of Ensuhkeshdanna's council advised him to comply with Enmerkar, he listened instead to a local priest, who promised to make Uruk subject to Aratta. When the priest arrived in Uruk, however, he was outwitted and killed by a wise old woman, Sagburru, and the two sons of the goddess Nidaba. After he learned the fate of his priest, Ensuhkeshdanna's will was broken and he yielded to Enmerkar's demands.

A third epic, *Lugalbanda and Enmerkar*, tells of the heroic journey to Aratta made by Lugalbanda in the service of Enmerkar. According to the epic, Uruk was under attack by Semitic nomads. In order to save his domain, Enmerkar required the aid of Inanna, who was in Aratta. Enmerkar requested volunteers to go to Inanna, but only Lugalbanda would agree to undertake the dangerous mission. The epic concerns the events of Lugalbanda's journey and the message given him from Inanna for Enmerkar. Although obscure, Inanna's reply seems to indicate that Enmerkar was to make special water vessels and was also to catch strange fish from a certain river.

ERESHKIGAL

Ereshkigal, a goddess in the Sumero-Akkadian pantheon, was Lady of the Great Place (i.e., the abode of the dead) and in texts of the 3rd millennium BCE wife of the god Ninazu (elsewhere accounted her son); in later texts she was the wife of Nergal. Ereshkigal's sister was Inanna (Akkadian: Ishtar), and between the two there was great enmity. In the rendezvous of the dead, Ereshkigal reigned in her palace, on the watch for lawbreakers and on guard over the fount of life lest any of her subjects take of it and so escape her rule. Her offspring and servant was Namtar, the evil demon, Death. Her power extended to earth where, in magical ceremony, she liberated the sick possessed of evil spirits.

Ereshkigal's cult extended to Asia Minor, Egypt, and southern Arabia. In Mesopotamia the chief temple known to be dedicated to her was at Cuthah.

SACRED CALENDARS

During most of the 2nd millennium BCE each major Mesopotamian city had its own calendar. The months were named from local religious festivals celebrated in the month in question. Only by the 2nd millennium BCE did the Nippur calendar attain general acceptance. The nature of the festivals in these various sacred calendars sometimes reflected the cycle of agricultural activities, such as celebrating the ritual hitching up of the plows and, later in the year, their unhitching, or rites of sowing, harvesting, and other activities. The sacred calendar of Girsu at the end of the Early Dynastic period is rich in its accounting of festivals. During some of these festival periods the queen traveled through her domain to present funerary offerings of barley, malt, and other agricultural products to the gods and to the spirits of deceased charismatic human administrators.

The cycles of festivals celebrating the marriage and early death of Dumuzi and similar fertility figures in spring were structured according to the backgrounds of the various communities of farmers, herders, or date growers. The sacred wedding—sometimes a fertility rite, sometimes a harvest festival with overtones of

Third-millennium BCE cylinder seal illustrating the farming communities of the Akkadian people. Werner Forman/Universal Images Group/ Getty Images

thanksgiving—was performed as a drama: the ruler and a high priestess took on the identity of the two deities and so ensured that their highly desirable union actually took place. In many communities the lament for the dead god took the form of a procession out into the desert to find the slain god in his gutted fold, a pilgrimage to the accompaniment of harps and heart-rending laments for the god.

Of major importance in later times was the New Year festival, or Akitu, celebrated in a special temple out in the fields. Originally an agricultural festival connected with sowing and harvest, it became the proper occasion for the crowning and investiture of a new king. In Babylon it came to celebrate the sun god Marduk's victory over Tiamat, the goddess of the watery deep. Besides the yearly festivals there were also monthly festivals at new moon, the 7th, the 15th, and the 28th of the month. The last—when the moon was invisible and thought to be dead—had a distinctly funereal character.

GILGAMESH

Gilgamesh is the best known of all ancient Mesopotamian heroes. Numerous tales in the Akkadian language have been told about Gilgamesh, and the whole collection has been described as an odyssey—the odyssey of a king who did not want to die.

The fullest extant text of the Gilgamesh epic is on 12 incomplete Akkadian-language tablets found at Nineveh in the library of the Assyrian king Ashurbanipal (reigned 668–627 BCE). The gaps that occur in the tablets have been partly filled by various fragments found elsewhere in Mesopotamia and Anatolia. In addition, five short poems in the Sumerian language are known from tablets that were written during the first half of the 2nd millennium BCE; the poems have been titled "Gilgamesh and Huwawa," "Gilgamesh and the Bull of Heaven," "Gilgamesh and Agga of Kish," "Gilgamesh, Enkidu, and the Netherworld," and "The Death of Gilgamesh."

The Gilgamesh of the poems and of the epic tablets was probably the Gilgamesh who ruled at Uruk in southern Mesopotamia sometime during the first half of the 3rd millennium BCE and who was thus a contemporary of Agga, ruler of Kish; Gilgamesh of Uruk was also mentioned in the Sumerian list of kings as reigning after the Flood. There is, however, no historical evidence for the exploits narrated in poems and epic.

The Ninevite version of the epic begins with a prologue in praise of Gilgamesh, part divine and part human, the great builder and warrior, knower of all things on land and sea. In order to curb Gilgamesh's seemingly harsh

Eighth-century BCE Assyrian statue of Gilgamesh. DEA/G. Dagli Orti/
De Agostini/Getty Images

rule, the god Anu caused the creation of Enkidu, a wild man who at first lived among animals. Soon, however, Enkidu was initiated into the ways of city life and traveled to Uruk, where Gilgamesh awaited him. Tablet II describes a trial of strength between the two men in which Gilgamesh was the victor; thereafter, Enkidu was the friend and companion (in Sumerian texts, the servant) of Gilgamesh. In Tablets III–V the two men set out together against Huwawa (Humbaba), the divinely appointed guardian of a remote cedar forest, but the rest of the engagement is not recorded in the surviving fragments. In Tablet VI Gilgamesh, who had returned to Uruk, rejected the marriage proposal of Ishtar, the goddess of love, and then, with Enkidu's aid, killed the divine bull that she had sent to destroy him. Tablet VII begins with Enkidu's account of a dream in which the gods Anu, Ea, and Shamash decided that he must die for slaying the bull. Enkidu then fell ill and dreamed of the "house of dust" that awaited him. Gilgamesh's lament for his friend and the state funeral of Enkidu are narrated in Tablet VIII. Afterward, Gilgamesh made a dangerous journey (Tablets IX and X) in search of Utnapishtim, the survivor of the Babylonian Flood, in order to learn from him how to escape death. He finally reached Utnapishtim, who told him the story of the Flood and showed him where to find a plant that would renew youth (Tablet XI). But after Gilgamesh obtained the plant, it was seized by a serpent, and Gilgamesh unhappily returned to Uruk. An appendage to the epic, Tablet XII, related the loss of objects called *pukku* and *mikku* (perhaps "drum" and "drumstick") given to Gilgamesh by Ishtar. The epic ends with the return of the spirit of Enkidu, who promised to recover the objects and then gave a grim report on the underworld.

ISHKUR

Ishkur was the Sumerian god of the rain and thunder-storms of spring. He was the city god of Bit Khakhuru (perhaps to be identified with modern Al-Jidr) in the central steppe region.

Ishkur closely resembled Ninhar (Ningubla) and as such was visualized in the form of a great bull. He was the son of Nanna (Akkadia: Sin), the moon god. When portrayed in human shape, he often holds his symbol, the lightning fork. Ishkur's wife was the goddess Shala. In his role as god of rain and thunder, Ishkur corresponded to the Sumerian deities Asalluhe and Ninurta. He was identified by the Akkadians with their god of thunderstorms, Adad.

ISHTAR

I shtar (Sumerian: Inanna) was the goddess of war and sexual love. Ishtar is the Akkadian counterpart of the West Semitic goddess Astarte. Inanna, an important goddess in the Sumerian pantheon, came to be identified with Ishtar, but it is uncertain whether Inanna is also of Semitic origin or whether, as is more likely, her similarity to Ishtar caused the two to be identified. In the figure of Inanna several traditions seem to have been combined: she is sometimes the daughter of the sky god An, sometimes his wife; in other myths she is the daughter of Nanna, god of the moon, or of the wind god, Enlil. In her earliest manifestations she was associated with the storehouse and thus personified as the goddess of dates, wool, meat, and grain; the storehouse gates were her emblem. She was also the goddess of rain and thunderstorms—leading to her association with An, the sky god—and was often pictured with the lion, whose roar resembled thunder. The power attributed to her in war may have arisen from her connection with storms. Inanna was also a fertility figure, and, as goddess of the storehouse and the bride of the god Dumuzi-Amaushumgalana, who represented the growth and fecundity of the date palm, she was characterized as young, beautiful, and impulsive—never as helpmate or mother. She is sometimes referred to as the Lady of the Date Clusters.

Ishtar's primary legacy from the Sumerian tradition is the role of fertility figure; she evolved, however, into a more complex character, surrounded in myth by death and disaster, a goddess of contradictory connotations and

Third-millennium BCE *Sumerian alabaster statue representing Ishtar.* DEA/G. Dagli Orti/De Agostini/Getty Images

forces—fire and fire-quenching, rejoicing and tears, fair play and enmity. The Akkadian Ishtar is also, to a greater extent, an astral deity, associated with the planet Venus. With Shamash, the sun god, and Sin, the moon god, she forms a secondary astral triad. In this manifestation her symbol is a star with 6, 8, or 16 rays within a circle. As goddess of Venus, delighting in bodily love, Ishtar was the protectress of prostitutes and the patroness of the ale-house. Her popularity was universal in the ancient Middle East, and in many centres of worship she probably subsumed numerous local goddesses. In later myth she was known as Queen of the Universe, taking on the powers of An, Enlil, and Enki.

KINGU

Kingu, in Babylonian mythology, was the consort of Tiamat. The creation epic *Enuma elish* tells how Tiamat, determined to destroy the other gods, created a mighty army and set Kingu at its head. When Kingu saw Marduk coming against him, however, he fled. After Tiamat's defeat, Kingu was taken captive and executed; the god Enki (Ea) created humans from his blood.

RELIGIOUS ART AND ICONOGRAPHY IN MESOPOTAMIA

The earliest periods in Mesopotamia have yielded figurines of clay or stone, some of which may represent gods or demons; certainty of interpretation in regard to these figurines is, however, difficult to attain. With the advent of the Protoliterate period toward the end of the 4th millennium BCE, the cylinder seal came into use. In the designs on these seals—often, it would seem, copies from monumental wall paintings now lost—ritual scenes and divine figures, recognizable from what is known about them in historical times, make their first appearance. To this period also belongs the magnificent Uruk Vase, with its representation of the sacred marriage rite. Until the early centuries of the 2nd millennium BCE the cylinder seal remains one of the most prolific sources of religious motifs and

Glazed tile relief of lions from the Ishtar Gate in Babylon. Iain Masterton/Photographer's Choice/Getty Images

representations of divine figures, but larger reliefs, wall paintings, and sculpture in the round greatly add to modern historians' understanding of who and what is rendered.

In the 2nd and 1st millennia BCE the humble categories of clay plaques and clay figurines often contained representations of deities, and the numerous sculptured boundary stones (*kudurrus*) furnish representations of symbols and emblems of gods, at times identified by labels in cuneiform. To the 1st millennium BCE belong also the magnificent colossal statues of protective genies (spirits) in the shape of lions or human-headed bulls that guarded the entrances to Assyrian palaces, and also, on the gates of Nebuchadrezzar's (died 562 BCE) Babylon, the reliefs in glazed tile of lions and dragons that served the same purpose.

KUBABA

Kubaba was the goddess of the ancient Syrian city of Carchemish. In religious texts of the Hittite empire (c. 1400–c. 1190 BCE), she played a minor part and appeared mainly in a context of Hurrian deities and rituals. After the downfall of the empire her cult spread westward and northward, and she became the chief goddess of the successor kingdoms (the neo-Hittite states) from Cilicia to the Halys River.

Kubaba was represented as a dignified figure draped in a long robe, either standing or seated, and holding a mirror. Although her name was adopted by the Phrygians for their great mother goddess in the form of Cybebe (Cybele), the Phrygian goddess bore little resemblance to Kubaba in other respects.

Ninth-century BCE *representation of Kubaba.* Danita Delimont/Gallo Images/Getty Images

KUSHUKH

Kushukh, also spelled Kushuh, was the Hurrian moon god. In the Hurrian pantheon, Kushukh was regularly placed above the sun god, Shimegi; his consort was Niggal (the Sumero-Akkadian Ningal). His home was said to be the city of Kuzina (location unknown), and his cult was later adopted by the Hittites. As Lord of the Oath he had as his special function the punishment of perjury. He was represented as a winged man with a crescent on his helmet and sometimes standing on a lion; in this form he appears among the images of Hittite gods at the rock sanctuary of Yazilikaya (near modern Bogazköy in Turkey).

LAHMU AND LAHAMU

In Mesopotamian mythology, Lahmu and Lahamu were the twin deities. They were the first gods to be born from the chaos that was created by the merging of Apsu (the watery deep beneath the earth) and Tiamat (the personification of the salt waters); this is described in the Babylonian mythological text *Enuma elish* (c. 12th century BCE).

Usually, Lahmu and Lahamu represent silt, but in some texts they seem to take the form of serpents, and, because the wavy line of a gliding snake is similar to the ripple of water, some scholars believe that Lahmu and Lahamu may have been only synonyms of Tiamat. Lahmu and Lahamu were rather vague deities who do not seem to have played any significant part in subsequent myths, although they may have been the progenitors of Anshar and Kishar.

MARDUK

Marduk, in Mesopotamian religion, was the chief god of the city of Babylon and the national god of Babylonia; as such, he was eventually called simply Bel, or Lord. Originally, he seems to have been a god of thunderstorms. A poem, known as *Enuma elish* and dating from the reign of Nebuchadrezzar I (1124–03 BCE), relates Marduk's rise to such preeminence that he was the god of 50 names, each one that of a deity or of a divine attribute. After conquering the monster of primeval chaos, Tiamat, he became Lord of the Gods of Heaven and Earth. All nature, including man, owed its existence to him; the destiny of kingdoms and subjects was in his hands.

Marduk's chief temples at Babylon were the Esagila and the Etemenanki, a ziggurat with a shrine of Marduk on the top. In the Esagila the poem *Enuma elish* was recited every year at the New Year festival. The goddess named most often as the consort of Marduk was Zarpanitu.

Marduk's star was Jupiter, and his sacred animals were horses, dogs, and especially the so-called dragon with forked tongue, representations of which adorn his city's walls. On the oldest monuments Marduk is represented holding a triangular spade or hoe, interpreted as an emblem of fertility and vegetation. He is also pictured walking or in his war chariot. Typically, his tunic is adorned with stars; in his hand is a sceptre, and he carries a bow, spear, net, or thunderbolt. Kings of Assyria and Persia also honoured Marduk and Zarpanitu in inscriptions and rebuilt many of their temples.

Marduk was later known as Bel, a name derived from the Semitic word baal, or "lord." Bel had all the attributes

Boundary stone depicting Marduk. DEA/G. Dagli Orti/De Agostini/
Getty Images

of Marduk, and his status and cult were much the same. Bel, however, gradually came to be thought of as the god of order and destiny. In Greek writings references to Bel indicate this Babylonian deity and not the Syrian god of Palmyra of the same name.

NABU

Nabu was a major god in the Assyro-Babylonian pantheon. He was patron of the art of writing and a god of vegetation. Nabu's symbols were the clay tablet and the stylus, the instruments held to be proper to him who inscribed the fates assigned to men by the gods. In the Old Testament, the worship of Nebo is denounced by Isaiah (46:1).

Samsuditana, the last king of the 1st dynasty of Babylon (reigned 1625–1595 BCE), introduced a statue of Nabu into Esagila, the temple of Marduk, who was the city god of Babylon. Not until the 1st millennium BCE, however, did the relationship between Marduk and Nabu and their relative positions in theology and popular devotion become clear. Marduk, the father of Nabu, took precedence over him, at least theoretically, in Babylonia. But in popular devotion it was Nabu, the son, who knows all and sees all, who was chief, especially during the centuries immediately preceding the fall of Babylon. He had a chapel named Ezida in his father's temple Esagila, where at the New Year feast he was installed alongside Marduk. In his own holy city, Borsippa, he was supreme. At this time Nabu was also a prominent deity in Assyria, where several temples were devoted to his worship.

Goddesses associated with Nabu were Nana, a Sumerian deity; the Assyrian Nissaba; and the Akkadian Tashmetum, queen of Borsippa, stepdaughter of Marduk, and, as her abstract Akkadian name indicates, Lady of Hearing and of Favour. She was rarely invoked apart from her husband, Nabu, whose name means "speaking." Thus, while Nabu speaks, Tashmetum listens.

Ninth-century BCE stone relief with cuneiform script depicting the sun god Shamash (right) receiving Nabu, standing between two deities. Iberfoto/SuperStock

NERGAL

Nergal, in Mesopotamian religion, was a secondary god of the Sumero-Akkadian pantheon. He was identified with Irra, the god of scorched earth and war, and with Meslamtaea, He Who Comes Forth from Meslam. Cuthah (modern Tall Ibrahim) was the chief centre of his cult. In later thought he was a "destroying flame" and had the epithet sharrapu ("burner"). Assyrian documents of the 1st millennium BCE describe him as a benefactor of men, who hears prayers, restores the dead to life, and protects agriculture and flocks. Hymns depict him as a god of pestilence, hunger, and devastation.

The other sphere of Nergal's power was the underworld, of which he became king. According to one text, Nergal, escorted by demons, descended to the underworld where the goddess Ereshkigal (or Allatum) was queen. He threatened to cut off her head, but she saved herself by becoming his wife, and Nergal obtained kingship over the underworld.

Nergal did not figure prominently in epics and myths, although he did have a part in the *Epic of Gilgamesh* and the Deluge story. The cult of Nergal was widespread beyond the borders of Sumer and Akkad, where it first appeared. He had a sanctuary at Mari (modern Tell al-Hariri), on the Euphrates. He is named in inscriptions of Assyrian kings, and evidence of his cult is found in Canaan and at Athens.

NINHURSAG

Ninhursag was the city goddess of Adab and of Kish in the northern herding regions; she was the goddess of the stony, rocky ground, the *hursag*. In particular, she had the power in the foothills and desert to produce wildlife. Especially prominent among her offspring were the onagers (wild asses) of the western desert. As the sorrowing mother animal she appears in a lament for her son, a young colt, but as goddess of birth she is not only the goddess of animal birth but the Mother of All Children, a mother-goddess figure. Her other names include: Dingirmakh (Exalted Deity), Ninmakh (Exalted Lady), Aruru (Dropper, i.e., the one who "loosens" the scion in birth), and Nintur (Lady Birth Giver). Her husband is the god Shulpae, and among their children were the sons Mululil and Ashshirgi and the daughter Egime. Mululil seems to have been a dying god, like Dumuzi, whose death was lamented in yearly rites.

ADMINISTRATION IN MESOPOTAMIA

In Mesopotamia, the supreme responsibility for the correct carrying out of the cult, on which the welfare of the country depended, was entrusted to the city ruler, or, when the country was united, the king. The city ruler and the king were, however, far more than administrators; they also were charismatic figures imparting their individual magic into their rule, thus creating welfare and fertility. In certain periods the king was deified; throughout the 3rd millennium BCE, he became, in ritual action, the god Dumuzi in the rite of the sacred marriage and thus ensured fertility for his land. All the rulers of the 3rd dynasty of Ur (c. 2112–c. 2004 BCE) and most of the rulers of the dynasty of Isin (c. 2020–c. 1800 BCE) were treated as embodiments of the dying god Damu and invoked in the ritual laments for him. As a vessel of sacred power the king was surrounded by strict ritual to protect that power, and he had to undergo elaborate rituals of purification if the power became threatened.

The individual temples were usually administered by officials called *sangas* ("bishops"), who headed staffs of accountants, overseers of agricultural and industrial works on the temple estate, and *gudus* (priests), who looked after the god as house servants. Among the priestesses the highest-ranking was termed *en* (Akkadian: *entu*). They were usually princesses of royal blood and were considered the human spouses of the gods they served, participating as brides in the rites of the sacred marriage. Other ranks of priestesses are known, most of them to be considered orders of nuns. The best-known are the votaries of the sun god, who lived in a cloister (*gagûm*) in Sippar. Whether, besides nuns, there were also priestesses devoted to sacred prostitution is a moot question; what is clear is that prostitutes were under the special protection of the goddess Inanna (Ishtar).

NINLIL

Ninlil was the consort of the god Enlil and a deity of destiny. She was worshiped especially at Nippur and Shuruppak and was the mother of the moon god, Sin (Sumerian: Nanna). In Assyrian documents Belit is sometimes identified with Ishtar (Sumerian: Inanna) of Nineveh and sometimes made the wife of either Ashur, the national god of Assyria, or of Enlil, god of the atmosphere.

The Sumerian Ninlil was a grain goddess, known as the Varicoloured Ear (of barley). She was the daughter of Haia, god of the stores, and Ninshebargunu (or Nidaba). The myth recounting the rape of Ninlil by her consort, the wind god Enlil, reflects the life cycle of grain: Enlil, who saw Ninlil bathing in a canal, raped and impregnated her. For his crime he was banished to the underworld, but Ninlil followed. In the course of their journey Enlil assumed three different guises, and in each incident he ravished and impregnated Ninlil. The myth seems to represent the process of wind pollination, ripening, and the eventual withering of the crops and their subsequent return to the earth (corresponding to Ninlil's sojourn in the underworld).

NINSUN

The Sumerian deity Ninsun was the city goddess of Kullab in the southern herding region. As Ninsun's name, Lady Wild Cow, indicates, she was originally represented in bovine form and was considered the divine power behind, as well as the embodiment of, all the qualities the herdsman wished for in his cows: she was the "flawless cow" and a "mother of good offspring that loves the offspring." She was, however, also represented in human form and could give birth to human offspring. The Wild Bull Dumuzi (as distinct from Dumuzi the Shepherd) was traditionally her son, whom she lamented in the yearly ritual marking his death. In her role as a mother figure, her other Sumerian counterparts include Ninhursag (Akkadian: Belit-ili) and Ninlil (Belit). Ninsun's husband was the legendary hero Lugalbanda.

NINURTA

In Mesopotamian religion, Ninurta was the city god of Girsu (Tal'ah, or Telloh) in the Lagash region. Ninurta was the farmer's version of the god of the thunder and rainstorms of the spring. He was also the power in the floods of spring and was god of the plow and of plowing. Ninurta's earliest name was Imdugud (now also read as Anzu), which means "Rain Cloud," and his earliest form was that of the thundercloud envisaged as an enormous black bird floating on outstretched wings roaring its thunder cry from a lion's head. With the growing tendency toward anthropomorphism, the old form and name were gradually disassociated from the god as merely his emblems; enmity toward the older unacceptable shape eventually made it evil, an ancient enemy of the god.

Ninurta was the son of Enlil and Ninlil (Belit) and was married to Bau, in Nippur called Ninnibru, Queen of Nippur. A major festival of his, the Gudsisu Festival, marked in Nippur the beginning of the plowing season.

THE MAGICAL ARTS

In the ancient Mesopotamian view, gods and humans shared one world. The gods lived among men on their great estates (the temples), ruled, upheld law and order for humans, and fought their wars. In general, knowing and carrying out the will of the gods was not a matter for doubt: they wanted the practice of their cult performed faultlessly and work on their estates done willingly and well, and they disapproved, in greater or lesser degree, of breaches of the moral and legal order. On occasion, however, humans might well be uncertain: Did a god want his temple rebuilt or did he not? In all such cases and others like them, the Mesopotamians sought direct answers from the gods through divination, or, conversely, the gods might take the initiative and convey specific wishes through dreams, signs, or portents.

There were many forms of divination. Of interest to students of biblical prophecy is recent evidence that prophets and prophetesses were active at the court of Mari on the Euphrates in Old Babylonian times (c. 1800–c. 1600 BCE). In Mesopotamia as a whole, however, the forms of divination most frequently used seem to have been incubation—sleeping in the temple in the hope that the god would send an enlightening dream—and hepatoscopy—examining the entrails, particularly the liver, of a lamb or kid sacrificed for a divinatory purpose, to read what the god had "written" there by interpreting variations in form and shape. In the 2nd and 1st millennia BCE large and detailed handbooks in hepatoscopy were composed for consultation by the diviners. Though divination in historical times was regularly presented in terms of ascertaining the divine will, there are internal indications in the materials suggesting that it was originally less theologically elaborated. Apparently it was a mere attempt to read the future from "symptoms" in the present, much as a physician recognizes the onset of a disease. This is particularly evident in that branch of divination that deals with unusual happenings believed to be ominous. Thus, if a desert plant sprouted in a city—indicating that desert essence was about to take over—it was considered an indication that the city would be laid waste.

Related to the observation of unusual happenings in society or nature, but far more systematized, was astrology. The movements and appearance of the Sun, the Moon, and the planets were believed to yield information about future events affecting the nation or, in some cases, the fate of individuals. Horoscopes, predicting the character and fate of a person on the basis of the constellation of the stars at his birth, are known to have been constructed in the late 1st millennium BCE, but the art may conceivably be older.

Witchcraft was apparently at all times considered a crime punishable by death. Frequently, however, it probably was difficult to identify the witch in individual cases, or even to be sure that a given evil was the result of witchcraft rather than of other causes. In such cases, the expert in white magic, the *āšipu* or *mašmašu*, was able to help both in diagnosing the cause of the evil and in performing the appropriate rituals and incantation to fight it off. In earlier times the activities of the magicians seem generally to have been directed against the lawless demons who attacked humans and caused all kinds of diseases. In the later half of the 2nd, and all through the 1st millennium BCE, however, the fear of man-made evils grew, and witchcraft vied with the demons as the chief source of all ills.

SHAMASH

Shamash was the god of the sun, who, with the moon god, Sin (Sumerian: Nanna), and Ishtar (Sumerian: Inanna), the goddess of Venus, was part of an astral triad of divinities. Shamash was the son of Sin.

Shamash, as the solar deity, exercised the power of light over darkness and evil. In this capacity he became known as the god of justice and equity and was the judge of both gods and men. (According to legend, the Babylonian king Hammurabi received his code of laws from Shamash.) At night, Shamash became judge of the underworld.

Shamash was not only the god of justice but also governor of the whole universe; in this aspect he was pictured seated on a throne, holding in his hand the symbols of justice and righteousness, a staff and a ring. Also associated with Shamash is the notched dagger. The god is often pictured with a disk that symbolized the Sun.

As the god of the sun, Shamash was the heroic conqueror of night and death who swept across the heavens on horseback or, in some representations, in a boat or chariot. He bestowed light and life. Because he was of a heroic and wholly ethical character, he only rarely figured in mythology, where the gods behaved all too often like mortals. The chief centres of his cult were at Larsa in Sumer and at Sippar in Akkad. Shamash's consort was Aya, who was later absorbed by Ishtar.

Babylonian stela bearing the Code of Hammurabi and illustrating the king receiving the laws from Shamash. DEA/G. Dagli Orti/De Agostini/Getty Images

SACRED PLACES OF WORSHIP IN MESOPOTAMIA

Mesopotamian worshippers might worship in open-air sanctuaries, chapels in private houses, or small separate chapels located in the residential quarters of town, but the sacred place par excellence was the temple. Archaeology has traced the temple back to the earliest periods of settlement, and though the very early temple plans still pose many unsolved problems, it is clear that from the Early Dynastic period onward the temple was what the Sumerian (*e*) and Akkadian (*bītum*) terms for it indicate; i.e., the temple was the god's house or dwelling. In its more elaborate form such a temple would be built on a series of irregular artificial platforms, one on top of the other; by the 3rd dynasty of Ur, near the end of the 3rd millennium BCE, these became squared off to form a ziggurat. On the lowest of these platforms a heavy wall—first oval, later rectangular—enclosed storerooms, the temple kitchen, workshops, and other such rooms. On the highest level, approached by a stairway, were the god's living quarters centred in the cella, a rectangular room with an entrance door in the long wall near one corner. The god's place was on a podium in a niche at the short wall farthest from the entrance; benches with statues of worshippers ran along both long walls, and a hearth in the middle of the floor served for heating. Low pillars in front of the god's seat seem to have served as supports for a hanging that shielded the god from profane eyes. Here, or in a connecting room, would be the god's table, bed, and bathtub.

At a later time in Babylonia the cella with its adjoining rooms were greatly enlarged so that it became an open court surrounded by rooms. Only the section separated by the hanging remained roofed and became a new cella, entered from the middle of its long side and with the god in his niche in the wall directly opposite. The development in Assyria took a slightly different course. There, the original door in the long side moved around the corner to the short side opposite the god, creating a rectangular cella entered from the end wall.

The function of the temple, as of all of the other sacred places in ancient Mesopotamia, was primarily to ensure the god's presence and

to provide a place where he could be approached. The providing of housing, food, and service for the god achieved the first of these purposes. His presence was also assured by a suitable embodiment—the cult statue, and, for certain rites, the body of the ruler. To achieve the second purpose, greeting gifts, praise hymns as introduction to petitions, and other actions were used to induce the god to receive the petitioner and to listen to, and accept, his prayers.

In view of the magnitude of the establishment provided for the gods and the extent of lands belonging to them and cultivated for them—partly by temple personnel, partly by members of the community holding temple land in some form of tenure—it was unavoidable that temples should vie in economic importance with similar large private estates or with estates belonging to the crown. This importance, one may surmise, would lie largely in the element of stability that an efficiently run major estate

Third-millennium BCE *Sumerian statue depicting a worshipping figure, excavated from the archaeological site of Mari.* DEA/A. Dagli Orti/ De Agostini/Getty Images

Representation of the Anu-Adad temple in Assur, one of the ancient capitals of Assyria. Culture Club/Hulton Archive/Getty Images

provided for the community. With its capacity for producing large storable surpluses that could be used to offset bad years and with its facilities for production—such as its weaveries—the temple estates could absorb and utilize elements of the population, such as widows, waifs, captives, and others, who otherwise would have perished or become a menace to the community in one way or other. The economic importance of the temple primarily was local. The amount of foreign trade carried on by temples apparently was small. The power behind foreign trade seems rather to have been the king.

SIN

In Mesopotamian religion, Sin was the god of the moon. Sin was the father of the sun god, Shamash (Sumerian: Utu), and, in some myths, of Ishtar (Sumerian: Inanna), goddess of Venus, and with them formed an astral triad of deities.

Nanna, the Sumerian name for the moon god, may have originally meant only the full moon, whereas Su-en, later contracted to Sin, designated the crescent moon. At any rate, Nanna was intimately connected with the cattle herds that were the livelihood of the people in the marshes of the lower Euphrates River, where the cult developed. (The city of Ur, of the same region, was the chief centre of the worship of Nanna.) The crescent, Nanna's emblem, was sometimes represented by the horns of a great bull. Nanna bestowed fertility and prosperity on the cowherds, governing the rise of the waters, the growth of reeds, the increase of the herd, and therefore the quantity of dairy products produced. His consort, Ningal, was a reed goddess. Each spring, Nanna's worshipers reenacted his mythological visit to his father, Enlil, at Nippur with a ritual journey, carrying with them the first dairy products of the year. Gradually Nanna became more human: from being depicted as a bull or boat, because of his crescent emblem, he came to be represented as a cowherd or boatman.

Sin was represented as an old man with a flowing beard—a wise and unfathomable god—wearing a headdress of four horns surmounted by a crescent moon. The last king of Babylon, Nabonidus (reigned c. 556–539 BCE), attempted to elevate Sin to a supreme position within the pantheon.

TAMMUZ

In Mesopotamian religion, Tammuz (Sumerian: Dumuzi) was the god of fertility embodying the powers for new life in nature in the spring. The name Tammuz seems to have been derived from the Akkadian form Tammuzi, based on early Sumerian Damu-zid, The Flawless Young, which in later standard Sumerian became Dumu-zid, or Dumuzi. The earliest known mention of Tammuz is in texts dating to the early part of the Early Dynastic III period (c. 2600–c. 2334 BCE), but his cult probably was much older. Although the cult is attested for most of the major cities of Sumer in the 3rd and 2nd millennia BCE, it centred in the cities around the central steppe area (the *edin*)—for example, at Bad-tibira (modern Madinah), where Tammuz was the city god.

As shown by his most common epithet, Sipad (Shepherd), Tammuz was essentially a pastoral deity. His father, Enki, is rarely mentioned, and his mother, the goddess Duttur, was a personification of the ewe. His own name, Dumu-zid, and two variant designations for him, Ama-ga (Mother Milk) and U-lu-lu (Multiplier of Pasture), suggest that he actually was the power for everything that a shepherd might wish for: grass to come up in the desert, healthy lambs to be born, and milk to be plentiful in the mother animals.

When the cult of Tammuz spread to Assyria in the 2nd and 1st millennia BCE, the character of the god seems to have changed from that of a pastoral to that of an agricultural deity. The texts suggest that in Assyria (and later among the Sabaeans), Tammuz was basically viewed as the power in the grain, dying when the grain was milled.

The cult of Tammuz centred around two yearly festivals—one celebrating his marriage to the goddess Inanna, the other lamenting his death at the hands of demons from the netherworld. During the 3rd Dynasty of Ur (c. 2112–c. 2004 BCE) in the city of Umma (modern Tell Jokha), the marriage of the god was dramatically celebrated in February–March, Umma's Month of the Festival of Tammuz. During the Isin-Larsa period (c. 2004–c. 1792 BCE), the texts relate that in the marriage rite the king actually took on the identity of the god and thus, by consummating the marriage with a priestess incarnating the goddess, magically fertilized and fecundated all of nature for the year.

The celebrations in March–April that marked the death of the god also seem to have been dramatically performed. Many of the laments for the occasion have as a setting a procession out into the desert to the fold of the slain god. In Assyria, however, in the 7th century BCE, the ritual took place in June–July. In the major cities of the realm, a couch was set up for the god upon which he lay in state. His body appears to have been symbolized by an assemblage of vegetable matter, honey, and a variety of other foods.

Among the texts dealing with the god is "Dumuzi's Dream," a myth telling how Tammuz had a dream presaging his death and how the dream came true in spite of all his efforts to escape. A closely similar tale forms the second half of the Sumerian myth "The Descent of Inanna," in which Inanna (Akkadian: Ishtar) sends Tammuz as her substitute to the netherworld. His sister, Geshtinanna, eventually finds him, and the myth ends with Inanna decreeing that Tammuz and his sister may alternate in the netherworld, each spending half of the year among the living.

Tammuz's courtship and wedding were a popular theme for love songs and anecdotal verse compositions that seem to have been used primarily for entertainment. A number of true cult texts, however, follow the rite step by step as if told by a close observer, and many laments were probably performed in the actual rites.

Eventually a variety of originally independent fertility gods seem to have become identified with Tammuz. Tammuz of the cattle herders, whose main distinction from Tammuz the Shepherd was that his mother was the goddess Ninsun, Lady Wild Cow, and that he himself was imagined as a cattle herder, may have been an original aspect of the god. The agricultural form of Tammuz in the north, where he was identified with the grain, may also have been an originally independent development of the god from his role as the power in the vegetation of spring. A clear fusion, though very early, was the merger of Tammuz in Uruk with Amaushumgalana, the One Great Source of the Date Clusters—i.e., the power of fertility in the date palm.

A later important fusion was the merger of Tammuz and Damu, a fertility god who probably represented the power in the sap of rising in trees and plants in spring. The relation of still other figures to Tammuz, such as Dumuzi-Apzu—a goddess who appears to have been the power in the waters underground (the Apzu) to bring new life to vegetation—is not entirely clear.

TESHUB

In the religions of Asia Minor, Teshub was the Hurrian weather god, assimilated by the Hittites to their own weather god, Tarhun. Several myths about Teshub survive in Hittite versions. One, called the "Theogony," relates that Teshubachieved supremacy in the pantheon after the gods Alalu, Anu, and Kumarbi had successively been deposed and banished to the netherworld. Another myth, the "Song of Ullikummi," describes the struggle between Teshub and a stone monster that grew out of the sea. Teshub's consort was Hebat (Queen of Heaven), and they had a son, Sharruma. In art, unless identified by name or associated with Hebat, Teshub is often indistinguishable from the Hittite Tarhun. At the rock sanctuary of Yazilikaya near the ancient Hittite capital, the leading god is named Teshub and is represented treading on the bowed necks of two mountain gods. In other representations he is shown as a standing figure carrying a *lituus* (a long crook) or driving a chariot drawn by bulls. He reappears in the Kingdom of Urartu as Tesheba, one of the chief gods, and in Urartian art he is depicted standing on a bull.

GLOSSARY

ardour Extreme vigour or energy.

astral Of, relating to, or coming from the stars.

canon A regulation or dogma decreed by a church council.

efficacious Having the power to produce a desired effect.

emigrate To leave one's place of residence or country to live elsewhere.

encomiast One that praises.

enmity Positive, active, and typically mutual hatred or ill will.

hallowed Holy or consecrated.

incantation A use of spells or verbal charms spoken or sung as a part of a ritual of magic.

inchoate Being only partly in existence or operation.

ineluctably Not to be avoided, changed, or resisted.

lament To mourn aloud.

lexical Of or relating to words or the vocabulary of a language as distinguished from its grammar and construction.

magnanimous Showing or suggesting a lofty and coura-geous spirit.

mnemonic Assisting or intended to assist memory.

monarch A person who reigns over a kingdom or empire.

omen An occurrence or phenomenon believed to portend a future event.

panegyric A eulogistic oration or writing.

pantheon The gods of a people.

penitential Showing sorrow for sins or faults.

pious Marked by or showing reverence for deity and devotion to divine worship.

polity The form of government of a religious denomination.

presuppose To require as an antecedent in logic or fact.

psalm A sacred song or poem used in worship.

repertoire A list or supply of dramas, operas, pieces, or parts that a company or person is prepared to perform.

subjugation To bring under control and governance as a subject.

suzerain A dominant state controlling the foreign relations of a vassal state but allowing it to control its own internal affairs.

FOR FURTHER READING

Bryant, Megan E. *Oh My Gods!: A Look-It-Up Guide to the Gods of Mythology*. New York, NY: F. Watts/ Scholastic, 2010.

Campbell, Joseph. *The Hero with a Thousand Faces*. Princeton, NJ: Princeton University Press, 1972.

Campbell, Joseph, Bill D. Moyers, and Betty S. Flowers. *The Power of Myth*. New York, NY: Anchor, 1991.

Dalley, Stephanie. *Myths from Mesopotamia: Creation, the Flood, Gilgamesh, and Others*. Oxford, England: Oxford University Press, 2008.

Dell, Christopher. *Mythology: The Complete Guide to Our Imagined Worlds*. New York, NY: Thames & Hudson, 2012.

Hamilton, Edith, and Christopher Wormell. *Mythology*. New York, NY: Back Bay, 2011.

Hamilton, Edith. *Mythology: Timeless Tales of Gods and Heroes*. New York, NY: Grand Central, 2011.

Harris, Stephen L., and Gloria Platzner. *Classical Mythology: Images and Insights*. New York, NY: McGraw-Hill, 2012.

Leeming, David Adams. *The Oxford Companion to World Mythology*. Oxford, England: Oxford University Press, 2005.

Lenardon, Robert J., and Michael Sham. *Classical Mythology*. New York, NY: Oxford University Press, 2011

Otfinoski, Steven. *All in the Family: A Look-It-Up Guide to the In-laws, Outlaws, and Offspring of Mythology*. New York, NY: Franklin Watts, 2010.

Thury, Eva M., and Margaret Klopfle Devinney. *Introduction to Mythology: Contemporary Approaches to Classical and World Myths.* New York, NY: Oxford University Press, 2009.

Wilkinson, Philip. *Myths & Legends.* New York, NY: DK Publishing, 2009.

Witzel, Michael. *The Origins of the World's Mythologies.* Oxford, England: Oxford University Press, 2012.

Web Sites

Due to the changing nature of Internet links, Rosen Publishing has developed an online list of Web sites related to the subject of this book. This site is updated regularly. Please use this link to access the list:

http://www.rosenlinks.com/ggmyt/meso

INDEX